Ayurvedic Cures for Common Diseases

A Complete Book of Ayurvedic Remedies

RADIANT HEALTH SERIES

No.	Title / Author	Price
1.	**Yogic Asanas and Pranayama for Health and Longevity** *(Illustrated)* *Swami Akshaya Atmanand*	50/-
2.	**Yoga for the Cure of Common Diseases** *(Illustrated)* *Dr. Lakshminarain Sharma*	50/-
3.	**Beauty and Body Book** *(Illustrated)* *Chho Dev*	85/-
4.	**Overcoming Rheumatism and Arthrits** *(Illustrated)* *Phyllis Speight*	65/-
5.	**Heart Disease — Prevention and Cure** *James C. Thomson*	65/-
6.	**The Complete Book of Eye Care** *Dr. M.S. Agarwal*	75/-
7.	**Magneto Therapy for Common Diseases** *(Illustrated)* *Dr. M.T. Santwani*	50/-
8.	**Choose the Sex of Your Child —The Natural Way** *Dr. (Mrs.) I.K. Barthakur*	50/-
9.	**Acupressure Therapy** *Astrid I Goosmann-Legger*	65/-
10.	**Yoga : Nine Week Course** *Dr. Vinod Verma*	95/-
11.	**Surya Chikitsa : Colour Therapy for Common Diseases** *Dr. Mohan Lal Kathotia*	50/-

Available at all leading bookshops and directly from:

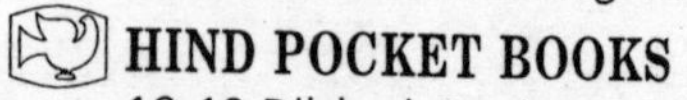

18-19 Dilshad Garden, G.T. Road, Delhi-110095
Tel. 2282467, 2297792, 93, 94 Fax. 2282332

Ayurvedic Cures for Common Diseases

A Complete Book of Ayurvedic Remedies

Dr. Bhagwan Dash

HIND POCKET BOOKS

Dedicated to
the Seekers of Truth and
o benefit all Manking

AYURVEDIC CURES FOR COMMON DISEASES
A Complete Book of Ayurvedic Remedies

Sixth paperback edition, 1999
ISBN 81-216-0074-X

Economy Paperback Edition

Published by
Hind Pocket Books (P) Ltd.
18-19, Dilshad Garden, G.T. Road
Delhi-110 095

Designing, Typesetting
& Print Production : SCANSET

18-19, Dilshad Garden, G.T., Road, Delhi-110 095
Tel: 228 2467, 229 7792, 93, 94 Fax: 228 2332

Printed at Balaji Offset, Delhi-110032

PRINTED IN INDIA

Contents

Introduction

THE WORD *Ayurveda* is composed of two terms, *Ayush* meaning life and *Veda* meaning knowledge or science. Thus, etymologically, Ayurveda means the science of life or biology. Medicine apart, various other aspects of life also come within the purview of Ayurveda. In its broader perspective it deals with the health and treatment of diseases of animals and even plants. Thus in ancient India, there were specialised subjects like *ashva-ayurveda* (for the treatment of horses), *gaja-ayurveda* (for the treatment of elephants); *go-ayurveda* (for the treatment of cows) and *vriksha-ayurveda* (for the treatment of diseases of plants). Treatises on these sciences were written by eminent scholars like Nakula, Shalihotra and Parashara.

Ayurveda provides rational means for the treatment of many internal diseases which are considered to be obstinate and incurable in other systems of medicine. Simultaneously it lays a great deal of emphasis upon the maintenance of positive health of an individual. It thus aims at both the prevention and cure of diseases. Ayurveda also studies basic human nature, and natural urges like hunger, thirst, sleep, sex, etc., and provides measures for a disciplined, disease-free life.

Practice of Ayurveda fell into disuse after repeated foreign invasions of India. Original works were destroyed, and quacks flourished who introduced unauthorised modifications in the system.

It was in late 19th century and the early 20th century that people started thinking afresh about the development of Ayurveda. This gained an impetus along with the *swadeshi* movement. Many expert committees were constituted by the Government to look into the problems of this science and suggest measures to solve them. After independence, the national Government took keen interest to set the affairs of Ayurveda on scientific lines and develop it because of which Ayurvedic colleges, dispensaries, hospitals and pharmacies were established in different parts of the country.

This handbook provides a general survey of the theory and practice of Ayurveda. Meant for the common householder, the emphasis is on home treatment for general complaints. The theory part of the book is therefore short and non-technical. It is my earnest hope that readers would find this edition useful in their daily life.

New Delhi **BHAGWAN DASH**

CHAPTER 1

FUNDAMENTAL PRINCIPLES OF AYURVEDA

THE HUMAN body according to Ayurveda, is composed of three fundamental elements called *doshas, dhatus* and *malas.* The *doshas* govern the physico-chemical and physiological activities of the body, while the *dhatus* enter into the formation of a basic structure of a body cell, thereby performing some specific actions. The *malas are* substances which are partly utilised in the body and partly excreted in a modified form after serving their physiological functions. These three elements are said to be in a dynamic equilibrium with each other for the maintenance of health. Any imbalance or their relative preponderance in the body results in disease and decay.

Pancha Mahabhutas: The man has five senses and through these senses he perceives the external world in five different ways. The sense organs are the ears, the skin, the eyes, the tongue and the nose. Through these sense organs, the external object is not only perceived, but also absorbed into the human body in the form of energy. These five types of senses are the basis on which the entire universe is divided, grouped or classified in five different ways, and they are known as five *mahabhutas.* They are named as *akasha* (sky), *vayu* (air), *agni* (fire), *jala* (water) and *prithvi* (earth). The English equivalents, however, do not connote the correct and full implications of these terms. For example, ordinary water does not contain *jala mahabhuta* alone, it is composed of all the five *mahabhutas.* It is the force of cohesion or the power of attraction that is inherent in *jala* or water which is the characteristic feature of *jala mahabhuta.* Similarly, air is not *vayu mahabhuta* alone, it contains the elements which belong to other *mahabhutas* also. For example, oxygen will be nearer to *agni mahabhuta* and hydrogen nearer to *jala mahabhuta.*

Modern physics and chemistry have divided the matter available in the universe into some basic elements. These elements differ from each other in certain respects. All these elements can be classified into five categories of *mahabhutas*. On the other hand, each atom has the characteristic features of all the five *mahabhutas* in it. The electrons, positrons, neutrons, etc., present inside the atom, represent *prithvi mahabhuta*. The force or cohesion because of which they remain attracted towards each other is the characteristic attribute of *jala mahabhuta*. The energy that is produced inside the atom when it is broken and the energy which remains latent in it in its unbroken form, represent the attributes of *agni mahabhuta*. The force of movement of the electrons represents the characteristic feature of *vayuv mahabhuta* and the space in which they move is the primary attribute of *akasha mahabhuta*.

Different schools of philosophy have tried to explain the *pancha mahabhuta* theory in different ways. While some of these explanations are basically the same, others are widely different. However, all schools of theistic philosophy have a common ground in their belief in the creation of this universe through the *pancha mahabhutas*. Some atheist schools of philosophy like the one of Charvaka does not believe in the existence of the fifth *mahabhuta*, i.e., *akasha* because, it is not perceptible to the ordinary eye. However, Ayurveda is very clear about it and believes in *pancha mahabhuta* theory.

According to Ayurveda, the body of an individual is composed of five *mahabhutas*. Similarly, in other extraneous matters, there are also five *mahabhutas*. In the human body, these five *mahabhutas* are represented in the form of *doshas, dhatus* and *malas*. Outside the body they form the basic ingredients of the drugs and food ingredients. The characteristic attributes of these five *mahabhutas* are explained in terms of *rasa* or taste, *guna* or quality, *virya* (potency) and *vipaka* (the taste that arises after the digestion and metabolism of a substance).

In a normal body of a living being, these substances remain in a particular proportion. However, because of enzymatic action inside the human body, this ratio of five *mahabhutas* or their equilibrium inside the body gets disturbed. The body has, however, a natural tendency to maintain equilibrium. It eliminates some of the *mahabhutas* which are in excess and takes some of the *mahabhutas* which are in shortage. This shortage of *mahabhutas* is replenished through the ingredients of food, drinks, air, heat, sunlight, etc. How the exogenous *pancha mahabhutas* are converted into indigenous *pancha mahabhutas* will be discussed at a later stage.

Even during the process of death, these five *bhutas* play a very important role. They have two different forms, namely, gross and subtle. The five categories of subtle *bhutas* inside the body impregnate the five senses for five times and thereafter, they get detached from these five senses and thus death occurs. The dead body loses the five senses and is composed, therefore, only of the five *mahabhutas.*

Tridosha Concept: As has been stated before, inside the body there are three *doshas* which govern the physico-chemical and physiological activities. These three *doshas* are *vayu, pitta* and *kapha.* The nearest English equivalents of these terms will be air, bile and phlegm.

As has been stated before, all the constituents of the body are derived from the five *mahabhutas.* Therefore, the *doshas* are also composed of five *mahabhutas.* All the *doshas* have all the five *mahabhutas* in their composition. The *vayu dosha* is dominated by *akasha mahabhuta* and *vayu mahabhuta.* In *pitta, agni mahabhuta* is predominant, and *kapha* is primarily constituted of *jala* and *prithvi mahabhutas.*

The doctrine of the *doshas* plays an important part in Ayurveda inasmuch as it forms the basis for the maintenance of positive health and diagnosis, as well as treatment of diseases. A correct appreciation of this doctrine is, therefore, essential for proper comprehension and appreciation of the theory and practice of Ayurveda. When they are in their normal state, they sustain the body and any disturbance in their equilibrium results in disease and decay. These three *doshas* pervade all over the body. There are, however, some elements or organs of the body in which they are primarily located. For example, the urinary bladder, the intestines, the pelvic region, the thighs, legs and the bones are the primary seats of *vayu.* The seats of *pitta* are the sweat, the lymph, the blood and the stomach. Similarly, the seats of *kapha* are the thorax, the head, the neck, the joints, the upper portion of the stomach and the fat tissues of the body. Each of these three *doshas* are again divided into five each. These five divisions represent only five different aspects of the same *doshas* and it should be made clear that they are not five different entities in the body.

Locations and functions of these divisions of *vayu*, *pitta* and *kapha* are given in the statement below:

Doshas	*Location*	*Normal function*	*Ailments caused by its vitiation*
A) *VAYU*			
1. *Prana*	Heart	Breathing and swallowing of food.	Hiccup, bronchitis, asthma, cold, hoarseness of voice.
2. *Udana*	Throat	Speech and voice	Various diseases of eye, ear, nose and throat.
3. *Samana*	Stomach and small intestines	Help in the action of digestive enzymes, assimilation of end-products of food and separation into their various tissue elements.	Indigestion, diarrhoea and defective assimilation
4. *Apana*	Colon and organs of pelvis.	Elimination of stool, urine, semen and menstrual blood.	Diseases of bladder, anus, testicles, obstinate urinary diseases including diabetes
5. *Vyana*	Heart	Helps in the functioning of circulating channels like blood vessels.	Impairment of circulation and diseases like fever, diarrhoea
B) *PITTA*			
1. *Pachaka*	Stomach and small intestines	Digestion	Indigestion

Doshas	*Location*	*Normal function*	*Ailments caused by its vitiation*
2. *Ranjaka*	Liver, spleen and stomach.	Blood formation	Anaemia, jaundice, etc.
3. *Sadhaka*	Heart	Memory and other mental functions.	Psychic disturbances.
4. *Alochaka*	Eyes	Vision.	Impairment of vision.
5. *Bhrajaka*	Skin	Colour and glaze of the skin.	Leucoderma and other skin diseases.
C) *KAPHA*			
1. *Kledaka*	Stomach	Moistens food which helps in digestion.	Impairment of digestion.
2. *Avalambaka*	Heart	Energy in limbs.	Laziness.
3. *Bodhaka*	Tongue	Perception of taste.	Impairment of taste.
4. *Tarpaka*	Heart	Nourishment of the sense organs.	Loss of memory and impairment of the functions of sense organs.
5. *Shleshaka*	Joints	Lubrication of joints	Pain in joints and impairment of the functions of the joint.

It will be seen from the above statement that the *doshas* and their divisions are located in almost all the vital organs of the body and regulate all the functions of both the body and the mind.

During different seasons of the year, these *doshas* undergo certain changes. For example, *vayu* gets aggravated during Juné-August, i.e., at the end of the summer. *Pitta* gets aggravated between October-December, i.e., during autumn, and *kapha* gets aggravated between February-April, i.e., during spring. If certain precautionary measures are not taken during these seasons the person would expose himself to certain diseases caused by these *doshas.* The precautions to be taken in these seasons will be described later. In the classical Ayurvedic texts, it is suggested that to promote positive health and prevent the occurrence of diseases, one should take medicated enema by the end of summer season, purgation during autumn and emesis or vomiting during spring.

Concept of Sapta Dhatu: The basic tissue elements of the body are known as *dhatus* in Ayurveda. The term *dhatu* etymologically means, one which assists the body or which enters into the formation of the basic structure of the body as a whole. The *dhatus* are seven in number and they are:

1) *Rasa* or chyle, including lymph, 2) *Rakta* or the haemoglobin fraction of the blood, 3) *Mamsa* or muscle tissue, 4) *Medas* or fat tissue, 5) *Asthi* or bone tissue, 6) *Majja* or bone marrow, and 7) *Shukra* or the sperm in male and ovum in female.

These seven *dhatus* are composed of the five *mahabhutas. Prithvi mahabhuta* predominates in muscle and fat tissues, *jala mahabhuta* predominates in the lymph and chyle, the haemoglobin fraction of the blood is primarily constituted of *tejas mahabhuta.* The bone is composed of *vayu mahabhuta* and the pores inside the bone are dominated by *akasha mahabhuta.* It should be made clear here again that all the seven *dhatus* are composed of all the five *mahabhutas* and only the dominating *mahabhutas* are described above. These *dhatus* remain inside the human body of the individual in a particular proportion, and any change in their equilibrium leads to disease and decay.

Concept of *Mala*: Stool, urine and sweat are the three important *malas* recognised in Ayurveda. They are the waste products of the body and their proper elimination is essential for the maintenance of the health of the individual. As is commonly believed, stool is not only the refuse of the food taken by the individual, but it also contains substances which are eliminated from the tissue cells of the body. Proper evacuation of stool is, therefore, essential for maintaining the tissue cells in their state of excellent health. If there is improper evacuation, diseases occur not only in the gastrointestinal tract, but also in other parts of the body. In diseases like lumbago, rheumatism, sciatica and paralysis and even bronchitis and asthma, taking necessary precautions to ensure proper evacuation of the stool is essential before starting any Ayurvedic treatment. If not properly evacuated, it provides a congenial atmosphere for the growth of different kinds of intestinal worms, and these at times affect the growth of some of the friendly bacteria in the colon which help in the synthesis of some of the useful material for the body.

Urine is another waste product through which many body wastes are thrown out. Even though excessive passage of urine is considered as a disease, in Ayurveda it is always advised that the person should take adequate quantity of water, both in summer and winter, so as to pass minimum six times of urine during the daytime.

Sweating is essential for the maintenance of health of the skin. Proper exercise, therapies like fomentation and certain drugs help the individual to sweat through which lot of waste products of the body are eliminated.

Normally stool, urine and sweat have foul smell. But at times the smell becomes intolerable and the individual has to take certain medicines for correcting these foul odours.

Srotas or Channels of Circulation: The whole body is composed of several types of channels of circulation through which the basic tissue elements, the *doshas* and some of the waste products circulate or move from one place to another constantly and continuously. For the proper functioning of the body it is necessary that these channels of circulation should remain perfect and the process of circulation should go on uninterruptedly. One of the important functions of these channels is to carry the product of the food from the gastrointestinal tract and to make them available to the basic tissue elements, thus helping in their nourishment. In brief, they include all the bigger channels of the body like the gastrointestinal tract, arteries, the veins, the lymphatics and the genito-urinary tract which are macroscopic, and fine capillaries which are microscopic.

Ayurveda recognises 13 channels in the human body. These *srotas* or channels of circulation play an important role in the advent of a disease. If the movement or the circulation in these channels is stopped or impaired because of some external or internal factors, then, this results in the accumulation of the substance being carried in that particular channel and the metabolism of the tissue is affected, thus giving rise to immature or uncooked products. These uncooked products not only accumulate there, but may circulate throughout the body being diverted to other channels which are still functioning. They thus impair the activities of those channels which results in the manifestation of a disease. To keep the channels perfect or in a state of proper functioning, many prescriptions and prohibitions are given in Ayurvedic texts. The important ones are, timely taking of food, passing out of excreta, attending to natural urges of the body, and physical exercises.

Digestion and Metabolism: Food which comes from the external world to the body is to be broken up, absorbed and assimilated. A heterogeneous substance has to be made homogeneous. The factors responsible for these activities in the body are known as *agnis.* They represent various types of enzymes in the gastro-intestinal tract, in the liver and in the tissue cells themselves. When the *doshas* of the body are in the state of equilibrium, these *agnis* or enzymes function normally. When, however, there is any disturbance in this equilibrium, there is impairment in the functions of these *agnis.* The four states of the *agnis* are summarised below:

State of Agni	*Symptoms*	*Remarks*
(1)	(2)	(3)
1) *Vishamagni*	Sometimes digests slowly, sometimes normally and sometimes produces *adhamana* (distension of abdomen), *shula* (colicky pain),	An erratic state of *agni* arising as a result of the influence of *vata,* is the condition described as *vishamagni.* In this

Contd.

	udavarta (upward movement of *vayu* in the stomach) *atisara* (diarrhoea), *jathara* (ascites), *gaurava* (heaviness), *antrakujana* (gurgling sound in the intestines) *pravahana* (dysentery).	state, it sometimes helps the process of complete digestion and at other times produces distension of the abdomen, colic pain, constipation, dysentery, ascites, heaviness of the limbs and even loose motions.
2) *Tikshnagni*	Digests even large quantities of all too frequent meals: after digestion produces *gala shosha* and *daha* (parched throat), *oshtha shosha* and *daha* (parched lips), *talushosha* and *daha* (parched palate), and *santapa* (heat and burning sensation).	The action of *jatharagni* in this state is influenced predominantly by *pitta*. The *agni* in this condition is said to be excessively excited and hence it is known as *tikshnagni*. easily digests even a very heavymeal, in a very short space of time. It causes voracious hunger — a condition usually spoken of as *atyagni* (or *bhasmaka* by certain authorities). It makes possible for a glutton to digest his all too frequent meals.
3) *Mandagni*	Cannot digest, even normal diet properly	This is a state in which the action of

Contd.

	causing *udara gaurava* (heaviness of abdomen), *shiro gaurava* (heaviness of the head), *kasa* (cough), *shvasa* (dyspnoea), *praseka* (salivation), *chhardi* (emesis) and *gatra sadana* (weakness of the body).	*jatharagni* is considerably inhibited due to the dominant influence of *kapha.* Hence, this state of *agni* is known as *mandagni.* In this state, the *agni* is unable to digest and metabolise even a small quantity of otherwise easily digestible food.
4) *Samagni*	Properly digests the normal diet.	In the well equilibrated state of functioning of *tridoshas*, the *jatharagni* is also stated to function normally. This state of its function has been described as *samagni.* In other words, *jatharagni* ensures complete digestion of food ingested at the proper time without any irregularities, when *tridoshas* are in an equilibrated state of functioning.

The concept of *agni* of Ayurveda, which refers to the manifold functions ascribed to *pitta* is at once comprehensive. It not only includes chemical agencies responsible for *aharapachana* in the *kashtha* (corresponding to gastro-intestinal digestion), which leads to separation of *sarabhaga* (nutrient fraction) of the *ahara* (food) from the *kittabhaga* the indigestible or undigested residue of the food) but also metabolic events — energy synthesis and maintenance metabolism. In addition, it comprehends photo and chemo-synthetic processes. *Pachaka pitta* known variously as *jatharagni, koshthagni, antaragni, pachakagni* and *dehagni* while being located in its own place in an area between *amashaya* and *pakvashaya*, directly participates in the digestion of food and at the same time, lends support to and augments the functioning of the remaining *pittas* present elsewhere in the body, viz., *ranjaka, sadhaka, alochaka* and *bhrajaka*. It is held that the *pachaka pitta* contributes moieties of itself to the seven *dhatvagnis*, and supports and augments the function of the latter.

Different types of Agnis: Agnis are of 13 types, viz., *Jatharagni* (1), *Bhutagnis* (5) and *Dhatvagnis* (7). *Jatharagni* refers to the phenomenon of gastro-intestinal digestion. *Bhutagnis* help in the transformation of the external *mahabhutas* into internal ones. The function of the *bhutagnis* is to make the extraneous *mahabhutas* homologous. *Dhatvagnis* or enzymes are located in the tissue elements of the body. They help in the assimilation and transformation of the nutrient material received after the *bhutagnipaka* into substances homologous to the tissue elements.

Ayurveda lays great deal of emphasis on all these *agnis* and hence it is treated as synonymous with the physical body. Before starting the treatment of any disease, the defects in these *agnis* are located and efforts are made to correct them. Most of the medicines used in Ayurveda contain substances which stimulate functioning of these enzymes at different levels. Some elimination therapies are also prescribed in Ayurveda with a view to cleaning the channels of circulation and removing waste products accumulated there. This helps in proper functioning of the *agnis*.

In the young age, the state of *agni* is mild and as the age advances, the power of *agni* increases, thus resulting in better digestion and metabolism. This helps in increase in the size of the body. After the age of 40, the power of the *agni* remains stable till the individual attains the age of 60. After 60, the power of these *agnis* declines. The body tissues do not get their nutrition properly. They reduce in number, size and quality. This gives rise to the process of ageing.

When the individual dies the functioning of the enzymes stops. Through rejuvenation therapy an effort is always made to rejuvenate and revitalise these enzymes so that they could maintain or increase their activities. This will help in the prevention of old age and the diseases associated with it.

The food we take gets itself converted into different tissue elements and for all the tissue elements there is a fixed time. This time of conversion of the food ingredients and production of a particular type of tissue can be changed through medicines. For example, aphrodisiacs or sex stimulants enhance the production of sperm and ovum from the food ingredients if the *agni* or the enzymes are stimulated through certain agencies.

A disease is caused by the obstruction of the channels of circulation. The obstruction is caused by the accumulation of waste products. These waste products or the uncooked material can be converted or eliminated if the *agni* or the enzymes of that locality are stimulated. This is the role most of the Ayurvedic medicines play and this is how diseases are controlled and cured.

CHAPTER 2

PRINCIPLES OF AYURVEDIC TREATMENT

DOSHAS, NAMELY, *vayu, pitta* and *kapha* are spread all over the body. They regulate functions of every tissue cell and are present in each of them. When the sperm and the ovum unite in the uterus of the mother to form a zygote, the *doshas* present in them and outside them in the uterus cause certain characteristic features which in Ayurvedic parlance are known as *prakriti.* If all the *doshas* are in the state of equilibrium, it gives rise to a healthy foetus, and the child born of it leads a very healthy life. If the *doshas* are very much in a disturbed state, then it either prevents conception, or does not allow the zygote to grow, or results in malformations. If, however, one or two of these *doshas* are in excess, they give rise to a type of physical constitution and psychic temperament of the individual born out of it. These characteristic features of the body and the mind remain with the individual throughout his life. It does not change, and any change in it is indicative of death. Seven types of *prakriti* are recognised in Ayurveda with their specific characteristics.

For Ayurvedic treatment, knowledge of *prakriti* is very important. For example, a person of *vata prakriti* is always likely to get *vatika* type of diseases and in him diseases of other types do not give much trouble, or are easily curable. To prevent the occurrence of diseases, the individual having *vata prakriti* should always avoid such factors as would aggravate *vata* and resort to *vata*-alleviating food, drinks and regime. Food ingredients which are unctuous and hot are likely to suit him most whereas to a *pitta prakriti* man cold things will be more suitable. Similarly, while administering medicines, other things being equal, a *pitta prakriti* patient is to be given cooling medicine and a *kapha prakriti* patient is to be given heating medicine having bitterness, dryness, roughness, etc. Quinine, for example, can be safely given to a *kapha prakriti* person. It will not be very suitable for an individual having *vata prakriti* and it will be harmful if it is given to a patient having *pitta prakriti.*

Drug composition: Like other things in the universe, a drug is composed of the five *mahabhutas,* namely, *akasha, vayu, tejas, jala* and *prithvi.* From the physical appearance alone, it will be difficult to ascertain *bhautika* composition of a drug. It has to be ascertained on the basis of the taste of these drugs. For example, if a drug is having sweet taste, then it is to be inferred that it is predominated by *prithvi* and *jala* and *agni mahabhutas.* One having saline taste is dominated by *prithvi* and *agni mahabhutas,* one having pungent taste is dominated by *agni* and *vayu mahabhutas,* one having bitter taste is dominated by *vayu* and *akasha mahabhutas,* and one having astringent taste is dominated by *prithvi* and *vayu mahabhutas.*

As has been described before, the *doshas* in the body are also composed of these five *mahabhutas,* i.e., *kapha* is dominated by *prithvi* and *jala mahabhutas, pitta* is dominated by *agni mahabhuta* and *vayu* is dominated by *vayu and akasha mahabhutas.*

If a disease is caused by the aggravation of *kapha dosha,* then the individual should be given drinks and drugs which have less of *prithvi* and *jala mahabhutas,* but more of *agni, vayu* and *akasha mahabutas.* From out of these three *mahabhutas,* drugs having pungent, bitter and astringent taste (the latter is only partial) contain these three *mahabhutas.* Therefore, medicines having these tastes, namely, pungent, bitter and astringent, are administered to a patient having a disease dominated by *kapha dosha.* The same rule will govern the selection of drugs for disease caused by other *doshas* also.

The above is only a brief explanation of the action of Ayurvedic drugs. There are many other factors which are taken into consideration while selecting a drug. They are attributes (*gunas*), the potency (*virya*), the taste that comes out after the material is digested (*vipaka*) and the specific action (*prabhava*). All these factors inside the drug are interconnected and inter-dependent, because they represent different aspects of the *mahabhutas* of which the drug is composed.

CLASSIFICATION OF AYURVEDIC DRUGS

The Ayurvedic drugs comprise vegetable, animal and material products. They can be classified into five categories:

a) **Scientifically studied drugs:** Some single drugs and compound preparations, for example, *Sarpagandha* and *Yogaraja guggulu*, have been studied scientifically and the therapeutic claims made on their behalf have been verified. *Sarpagandha* is useful for high blood pressure and *Yogaraja guggulu* for rheumatism.

b) **Popular non-toxic drugs:** Some Ayurvedic medicines are popular for their therapeutic utility and non-toxic character. One such medicine is *Chyavanaprash*. *Amalaki* is the most important ingredient of this medicine which is useful in treating diseases of lungs like bronchitis.

c) **Effective but toxic drugs:** There are some drugs, for example, *Bhallatakavaleha*, which possesses known therapeutic value but which also produces severe toxicity if used indiscriminately. *Bhallataka* is the most important ingredient of this medicine which is used in the treatment of chronic and obstinate skin diseases.

d) **Drugs for rare use:** Some drugs, for example, *Shrivishnu taila*, though mentioned in Ayurvedic classics, are not in extensive use. Only physicians in certain regions of India use them and recognise their efficiency.

e) **Hereditary and patent drugs:** Some physicians have specialised in curing certain diseases. The formulae and methods of preparation of the drugs they administer are known only to them, or to the trusted members of their family. While some of the drugs are not effective as the claims made for them, some others are found to be very effective. In most cases, the physicians do not agree to disclose the formula.

NAMING A DRUG FORMULATION

The names of the drug formulations are usually based on the following six factors:

a) **Important ingredient:** Some preparations are named after the most important ingredient, for example, *Amalaki-rasayana.*

b) **Authorship:** The name of the sage or rishi who first discovered or patronised the formula is used in naming the drug, for example, *Agastya haritaki.*

c) **Therapeutic property:** The disease for which the formula was indicated is at times used in naming the preparation, for example, *Kusthaghna lepa.*

d) **The first ingredient of the formula:** The drug that heads the list in the formula is sometimes used in naming the preparation, for example, *Pippalyasava.*

e) **Quantity of drug:** The preparation is named after the quantity of the drug used, for example, *Shatpala ghrita.*

f) **Part of the plant:** The drug is named after the part of the plant used, for example, *Dashamula kashaya.*

PHARMACEUTICAL PROCESSES

In Ayurveda, different pharmaceutical processes are followed in the preparation of drugs. Besides helping isolation of the therapeutically active fraction of the drugs, these processes help make the medicines:

a) easily administrable;
b) tasteful;
c) digestible and assimilable;
d) therapeutically more effective;
e) less toxic and more tolerable; and
f) more preservable.

SHODHANA OR PURIFICATION

Some raw drugs are required to be used after *shodhana.* The literal meaning of the word *shodhana* is purification. But this is often misinterpreted to mean that the substance is rendered physically and chemically pure.

Shodhana, no doubt, brings about physical and chemical purity to some extent but at times more impurities are added to the substance during certain stages of the process. By such addition, the drug becomes less toxic and therapeutically more effective. Pure aconite, for example, cannot be administered so freely as *shodhita* aconite. Aconite, which is a cardiac depressant, becomes a cardiac stimulant after *shodhana*. Thus, the actual *shodhana* processes require a detailed study and the correctness of the drug preparations subject to these processes should be assessed by the therapeutic effect of the finished products.

Some gum resins, such as *guggulu* and some drugs containing volatile oils, such as *kushtha* are also said to undergo *shodhana* by boiling them with milk, *go-mutra*, etc. Boiling, however, reduces the volatile oil content of the drug which is supposed to be therapeutically very active.

THE RATIONALE OF USING METALLIC MEDICINES

Metals, minerals, gems and jewels are in use in the medicine since Vedic period. But they were used extensively during the post-Buddhist era. Several Buddhist saints carried out research and composed works on metallic medicines. Some of these metals, like mercury, lead and arsenic are known to be poisonous to the body and some of them do not get absorbed into the blood from the intestines. Therefore, all metals, minerals, gems and jewels are processed with the following aims in view:

a) to make them absolutely non-toxic:

b) to make them easily absorbable through the intestinal mucosa and to make them assimilable through the walls of the cells;

c) to enhance their therapeutic efficacy so that these could be administered in a very small dose;

d) to make their therapeutic effects broad based; and

e) to make them delicious.

For the above mentioned purposes, these metals, etc, are first of all made to undergo the process of *shodhana* (lit. purification). During this process, the molecules of the metal become fragile and non-toxic. This is done by boiling and triturating with several herbs and animal products. Thus, the inorganic metal is converted into an organic compound.

Thereafter, follows another process, which is called the *marana* (lit. killing). During this process, the metal is rubbed with several plants and animal products and calcined by exposure to strong heat. This process is repeated several times till the metal is reduced to a fine state of division. During each process, the metallic powder is thoroughly triturated to achieve this objective.

Finally, the metal is subjected to a process called *amritikarna* (converting it into ambrosia). Different methods of *shodhana*, *marana* and *amritikarna* are prescribed for different metals, minerals, gems and jewels. The final product is usually called *bhasma* or calcined powder. These are absolutely non-toxic, safe and useful. In addition to curing diseases, they help in the rejuvenation of the body and preservation as well as promotion of positive health. They are used only in a small dose therapeutically. The properties of these *bhasmas* (calcined powders) are entirely different from those of the raw metals, minerals, gems and jewels. They are frequently used in ayurvedic recipes along with vegetable and animal products because of the following:

a) they are effective in minimum dose;

b) they do not produce any bad taste; and

c) they produce their therapeutic effect by curing the disease quickly. Many obstinate and otherwise incurable diseases are amenable to these metallic preparations.

It is keeping these above mentioned facts in view, that the system of treatment with recipes containing metals, etc., is called *daivi chikitsa* (heavenly treatment). What to speak of ordinary diseases, even several ailments needing conventional surgery are amenable to these metallic preparations.

CHAPTER 3

DINACHARYA : THE REGIMEN DURING DAYTIME

ONE SHOULD get up from bed early in the morning, before sunrise. This is considered to be an auspicious time when the air is fresh and there is minimum noise in the atmosphere. One should offer prayers according to one's own religion or belief. Before actually leaving the bed one should think of one's programme during the day.

Cleaning the face: One should wash one's face with water immediately after getting up from the bed. This helps in the cleaning of the dirt accumulated in the eyes, nose and mouth during night and gives freshness. In winter season, luke-warm water can be used for this purpose.

Protecting eyesight: While washing the face, one should take a mouthful of water, keep the mouth closed and keeping the eyes open as far as possible, sprinkle cold water on them. Water should be sprinkled over the eyes. This is considered to be very useful for preserving and promoting eyesight. After sprinkling water, eyelids should be gently rubbed so that the eye-balls get a tender massage.

Drinking a glass of water: After washing the face and mouth, one should take a glass of water. This is prescribed for all seasons and on all days. This helps in the smooth passing of stool and urine. Some people are in the habit of taking bed tea for this purpose. The reflex action produced by bed tea is different from the one produced by the glass of cold water. The latter only produces pressure, thus stimulating the intestines to start their movement for evacuation. Tea being hot stimulates the intestines so strongly that its stimulating effect loses its significance after some days and the individual starts developing constipation. The caffeine content of the tea or coffee produces some adverse effect on the glands of the stomach and intestines which the cold water does not do. Besides, the cold water is a very good tonic for the body. Taking cold water is, however, prohibited if the individual is suffering from cold, cough or sore throat.

Evacuation of bowels: One should make a regular habit of evacuating bowels immediately after getting up from bed. If one does not feel the urge for it, there could be two reasons. Either the meals have not been properly digested, or the individual had inadequate sleep. The habit of taking a glass of cold water in the morning overcomes the difficulties caused by indigestion and inadequate sleep, and thus, the individual gets clear motion. People who think very much or those who are short-tempered, sensitive or wrathful, do get lot of wind in their stomach. This accumulates in the intestines during the night. Wind is also formed because of the intake of certain pulses and fried things. They are also formed if the individual does not take leafy vegetables and fruits in adequate quantities. Whatever the cause may be, when the wind is formed, it creates some obstruction in the bowel movement. One may feel that he has complete evacuation but after sometime, he gets the urge again. There are people who go to the toilet 3-4 times in the morning itself, before they are satisfied with their evacuation. This causes lot of inconvenience and in many cases, the evacuation remains incomplete which causes suppression of appetite, indigestion, headache, uneasy feeling, fatigue and sleeplessness. Wind, when formed in excess, puts pressure on the heart and may increase palpitation. It is, therefore, necessary for the individual to take necessary steps in his food, drinks and sleep, so that he gets a clear motion in the morning. However, if he has an urge for the second time, it should not be stopped per force. That will not be good for health.

Cleaning teeth: One should use the twig of *neem, babul* or any other tree which is astringent, pungent or bitter in taste. The top of the twig should be crushed to make it soft so that the gums are not affected. This removes the foul smell and tastelessness. It removes the dirt of the tongue, teeth and mouth.

Tongue scraping: Tongue scrapers, which should not be sharp edged and are curved, are available in metals like gold, silver, copper, tin and brass. The dirt deposited at the root of the tongue, obstructs expiration and gives rise to foul smell. So the tongue should be scraped regularly.

Use of nasal drops: One should inhale *Anu taila* during the rainy season, the autumn and the spring. One who practises nasal therapy according to the prescribed method, his eyes, nose and ears are not affected by any morbidity. His hair and beard never become grey and he never experiences falling of hair.

Gargles: Til oil gargling is beneficial for the strength of jaws, depth of voice, gustatory sensation and good taste for food. One used to such gargles never gets sore throat, cracked lips, offensive breath or toothache.

Application of oil on the head: One who applies til oil on his head regularly does not suffer from headache, baldness or greying of hair. The hair remains black, long and deep-rooted. The skin of his face becomes bright and induces sound sleep.

Oil drops in the ears: Ear diseases due to vitiated *vata*, tortiscollis, lock jaw, hardness of hearing and deafness are prevented if oil is regularly dropped into the ears.

Oil massage: *Vayu* dominates in the tactile sensory organ, and this sensory organ is lodged in the skin. The massage is exceedingly beneficial to the skin, so one should practise oil massage regularly. One who undergoes oil massage regularly, enjoys a good physique, strong and charming. By applying oil regularly, the onslaught of ageing is slackened.

Exercise: Physical exercise brings about lightness, ability to work, stability, resistance to discomfort and alleviation of *doshas*(specially *kapha)*. It stimulates the power of digestion.

But physical exercise in excess may cause exertion, exhaustion, consumption, thirst, bleeding from different parts of the body (*raktapitta*), *pratamaka* (a type of dyspnoea), cough, fever and vomiting.

Perspiration, enhanced respiration, lightness of the body, inhibition of the heart and such other organs of the body are indicative of the exercise being performed correctly.

Exercise is contra-indicated for persons who are emaciated due to excessive sexual activity, already exhausted, in grip of anger, grief, fear, and for persons having *vatika* constitution and profession of speaking too much. One should not do exercise while he is hungry and thirsty.

Bathing: Bathing is purifying, libidinal stimulant and life-giving: it removes fatigue, sweating and dirt. It brings about strength in the body and is an aid *par excellence* for the enhancement of *ojas.*

Dress: Wearing clean apparel adds to the bodily charm, reputation, longevity and prevents inauspiciousness. It brings about pleasure, grace, competence, and good looks.

Use of perfumes: Use of scents and garlands stimulates libido, produces good smell in the body, enhances longevity and charm. It gives corpulence and strength to the body; it is pleasing to the mind.

Use of ornaments: Wearing of gems and ornaments adds to the prosperity, auspiciousness, longevity and grace, and prevents dangers from snakes, evil spirits, etc. It is pleasant and charming. It is also conducive to *ojas.*

Care of hair and nails: The dressing and cutting of hair, beard (including moustaches) and nails, etc., add to the corpulence, libido, longevity, cleanliness and beauty.

Food: One should eat in proper quantity. The quantity of food to be taken again depends on the power of digestion (including metabolism).

The amount of food which, without disturbing the equilibrium of *dhatus* and *doshas* of the body, gets digested as well as metabolised in proper time, is to be regarded as the proper quantity.

Items of food like *shali, shashtika, mudga,* common quail, gray partridge, antelope, rabbit, Indian sambar, etc.; even though light in digestion by nature are to be taken according to the quantity prescribed. Similarly preparations of flour, sugarcane and milk, *til, masha* and meats of marshy and aquatic animals, even though heavy in digestion by nature, are also required to be taken in proper quantity.

The light food articles are predominant in the qualities of *vayu* and *agni,* and heavy ones in *prithvi* and *jala mahabhutas.* Therefore, according to their qualities, the light articles of food, being stimulants of appetite, are considered to be less harmful even if taken in excess of the prescribed quantity. On the other hand, heavy articles of food are by nature suppressors of appetite and harmful if taken in excess unless there is a strong power of digestion and metabolism achieved by physical exercise. If the food article is heavy, only three fourth or half of the stomach capacity is to be filled up. Even in the case of light food articles, excessive intake is not conducive to the maintenance of the power of digestion and metabolism.

Taken in appropriate quantity, food certainly helps the individual in bringing about strength, youthfulness, happiness and longevity without disturbing the equilibrium of *dhatus* and *doshas* of the body.

Use of collyrium: One should regularly apply the collyrium made of antimony because it is useful for the eyes. *Rasanjana* is to be applied once in every five or eight nights for lacrymation of the eyes.

Of all the *mahabhutas*, *tejas* dominate the eyes, so they are specially susceptible to *kapha*. Therefore, the therapy which alleviates *kapha* is good for keeping the vision clear.

A strong collyrium must not be applied to the eyes during the daytime as the eyes, weakened by drainage, will be adversely affected at the sight of the sun.

Smoking: In Ayurveda different types of cigars are prescribed for smoking. They are made of vegetable drugs and do not include tobacco or narcotics like cannabis.

Smoking cures heaviness of head, headache, rhinitis, hemicrania, earache, pain in the eyes, cough, hiccup, dyspnoea, obstruction in throat, weakness of teeth, discharge from the morbid ear, nose and eye, purulent smell from nose and mouth, toothache, anorexia, lock jaw, torticollis, pruritus, infective conditions, paleness of face, excessive salivation, impaired voice, tonsillitis, uvulitis, alopecia, greying of hair, falling of hair, sneezing, excessive drowsiness, loss of consciousness, and hypersomnia. It also strengthens hair, skull bones, organs and voice.

Eight times are prescribed for habitual smoking because *vata, pitta* and *kapha* get vitiated during these times. One should smoke after bathing, eating, tongue scraping, sneezing, brushing the teeth, inhalation of medicated material, application of collyrium and after sleep.

Study: One should not study if there is insufficient lighting, during an outbreak of fire, nor during the earthquake, nor during important festivals, nor during the fall of metcors, nor during the solar or lunar eclipse, nor on a new moon date and nor during the dawn or dusk. One should not study without being initiated by a teacher. While studying, one should not recite words incomplete in sounds nor in high voice nor in hoarse voice, nor without proper accents nor without proper morphological symmetry, neither too fast, nor too slowly, nor with excessive delay, nor with too high nor too low pitch.

Night meals: Food should be taken as early as possible at night. There should be sufficient gap between the time of intake of food and the time of going to bed. This will help in proper digestion of food which will result in good sleep also. The food should, as far as possible, be light and easily digestible.

Use of curd at night: Intake of curd at night is strictly prohibited. Curd is otherwise good for health. But it has a bad effect on the channels of circulation which are obstructed. This results in impairment of sleep and disturbances in mobilization, specially for patients who are suffering from asthma, bronchitis and rheumatism.

Sex: One should not indulge in sexual intercourse with a woman during her menses or a woman who is suffering from a disease or is impure or is having infection or a woman with an ugly appearance, or with bad conduct or manners or with the one devoid of skills. One should not indulge in sexual intercourse with a woman who is not friendly or has no passionate desire or is passionately attached to somebody else or is married to somebody else or a woman of another caste. Sexual activity in any organ other than the genital organ is prohibited, Sexual activities are also prohibited under sacred trees, in a public courtyard, on a cross-road, in a garden, in a cemetry, at a slaughter house, in water, in medical clinics or in the house of *brahmins* or teachers or in temples. Such activities are again to be avoided during dawn and dusk and on inauspicious days. Nor one should indulge in such activities while impure or without intense desire or without erection or without having taken food or with excessive intake of food or in an uneven place or while under the pressure of the urge for micturition, after exertion, after physical exercise, in fasts, having exhaustion and in places having no privacy. One should make a habit to take a glass of milk added with sugar after a sexual act.

CHAPTER 4

FEVERS

INFLUENZA

INFLUENZA is an infectious disease, marked by depression, distressing fever, acute catarrhal inflammation of the nose, larnyx and bronchi, neuralgic and muscular pains, gastro-intestinal disorder and nervous disturbances. It is caused by a filterable virus and often occurs in epidemic form.

It usually occurs during seasonal change. In Ayurveda it is called *vata-shalaishmika jwara.* In a normal individual, during the period of seasonal change, the equilibrium of *doshas,* viz., *vata, pitta* and *kapha* gets slightly disturbed due to the change in temperature, rains etc. But, if there is abnormality in the change of temperature and rainfall, then the equilibrium of *doshas* gets exceedingly disturbed which results in this disease. Persons with a constipative tendency, and morbidity of the nasal mucous membrane or throat are more prone to get this disease.

Since the disease is generally associated with gastric disorder, *pippali* (long pepper) is considered to be a useful drug for this condition. It should be powdered and half teaspoonful of this powder should be given to the patient mixed with honey (about two teaspoonfuls) and ginger juice (half teaspoon). This may be given three times a day. If this drug is administered on the first onset of fever, further rise of temperature is checked. This also promotes the resistance of the patient against the attacks of bronchitis and throat congestion.

Tulasi (Ocimum sanctum) is the other drug of choice for this condition. Leaves of this plant, mixed with an equal quantity of dried ginger powder form an excellent substitute for tea in this condition. This may be given by adding milk and sugar three to four times a day.

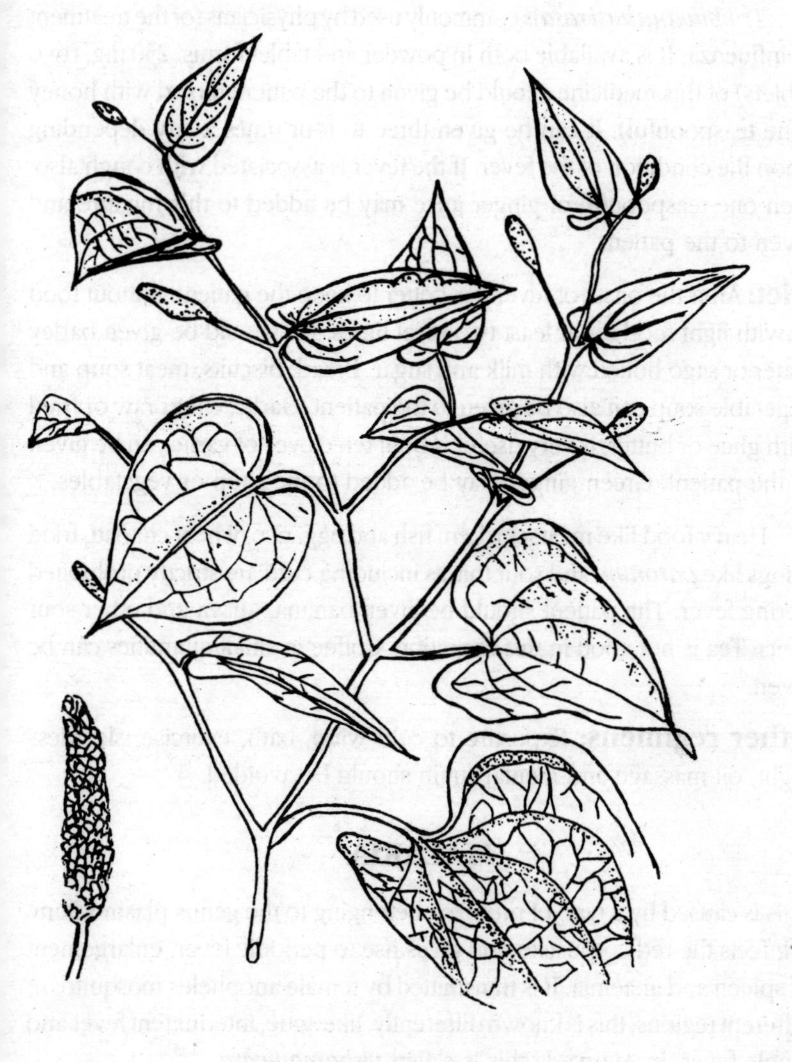

Fig. 1 *Piper longum* (*pippali*)

A simple but very effective remedy for this condition is *haridra* (turmeric). One teaspoonful of the powder or paste of this drug should be added to a cup of milk (to which sugar may also be added) and given to the patient three times a day. This brings about an early recovery. It cures malaise and removes constipation, if any. It keeps the lungs clear of phlegm and activates the liver.

Tribhuvana kirti rasa is commonly used by physicians for the treatment of influenza. It is available both in powder and tablet forms. 250 mg. (two tablets) of this medicine should be given to the patient mixed with honey (one teaspoonful). It can be given three to four times a day depending upon the condition of the fever. If the fever is associated with cough also, then one teaspoonful of ginger juice may be added to this mixture and given to the patient.

Diet: After the onset of fever it is better to keep the patient without food or with light food for at least two meal times. He should be given barley water or sago boiled with milk and sugar. Bread, biscuits, meat soup and vegetable soup can also be given to the patient. Garlic, either raw or fried with ghee or butter, is very useful. About ten cloves of garlic can be given to the patient. Green ginger may be added to the soup or vegetables.

Heavy food like meat, chicken, fish and egg, rice, wheat chapati, fried things like *parontha* and sour things including curd are strictly prohibited during fever. The patient should be given banana, guava and other sour fruits. Tea is not good in this condition. Coffee in small quantities can be given.

Other regimens: Exposure to cold wind, bath, exercise, sleepless night, oil massage and mental strain should be avoided.

MALARIA

This is caused by a type of protozoa belonging to the genus plasmodium. It infects the red corpuscles and gives rise to periodic fever, enlargement of spleen and anaemia. It is transmitted by female anopheles mosquito. In different regions, this is known differently, like ague, intermittent fever and jungle fever. In Ayurveda this is called *vishama jwara*.

Signs and symptoms: Prior to the manifestation of the disease, the patient may suffer from a transient headache, backache, generalised ache and tenderness in the liver area. There may be slight rise in temperature also. The onset of the fever is either sudden or slow. Prior to the fever, the patient may feel tiredness, stiffness of neck-muscles, pain in the muscles, bones and anorexia. Fever when it appears is generally associated with headache, backache, aching pains in the bones, malaise and fatigue. Usually in the beginning of the fever, there is shivering. But in certain types of malaria this shivering is absent. Nausea, anorexia and vomiting are very common. At the later stage of the disease, the spleen also gets enlarged. The fever is characterised by its remitting nature and is mostly associated with discomfort in the stomach region, bilious vomiting and chocolate colour stools. The onset of fever is generally in the morning or early afternoon. This fever is characterised by the following three stages:

a) **Cold stage:** The patient feels restless, develops headache, backache and experiences chilliness, then the shivering begins. The face is pinched and the skin turns cold and blue. Blankets and rugs are taken in an effort to keep warm. Nausea and vomiting during the onset of fever is not uncommon. In about half to two hours, the temperature rises rapidly up to 103^0F – 106^0F.

b) **Hot stage:** The skin becomes burning hot and all clothes and blankets are discarded. The face remains flushed and the pulse is rapid. The patient may get a headache and in severe cases, there may be delirium. This stage may persist for 8-10 hours.

c) **Sweating stage:** The skin becomes moist, followed by profuse sweating. The headache and pain disappear and the pulse becomes slow. The temperature then falls at the end of the attack, and the patient feels well.

Because of repeated attacks of the fever, in chronic cases the spleen becomes stony hard and enlarged. The patient becomes anaemic. When the patient becomes free from fever herpes appears on lips and face.

Treatment: *Sudarshana churna* is the drug of choice for the treatment of this disease. It is given to the patient in a dose of one teaspoonful, three times a day. To make it palatable, honey should be added and the whole thing made into a paste and administered to the patient. The important ingredient of *Sudarshana churna* is *Chirayata*. The powder of this drug is given to the patient in a dose of one teaspoonful, three times a day. This is also used in decoction form in a dose of six teaspoonfuls, three times a day. In all these preparations, honey is added.

Guduchi (Tinospora cordifolia) is often used for the treatment of this ailment. Six teaspoonfuls of the juice should be given to the patient three times a day. *Kutaja* is also useful in the treatment of malaria. The powder of this drug is given to the patient in a dose of one teaspoonful, three times a day, mixed with honey.

The treatment of the patient should be continued with these medicines even after he is free from fever. If used for sufficiently long time, it increases the immunity of the body against such attacks. Sometimes, the fever may get cured, but the splenic enlargement and anaemia may continue. The above mentioned medicines will be useful and this should be continued as long as the patient has even a trace of malaria.

Diet: During the attack phase and even thereafter, the patient usually suffers from loss of appetite. Food should not be given to the patient forcibly. Soups, barley water and milk can be given. When the patient is free from the attacks of fever, the appetite is restored. But even during this period, the patient should not be given the freedom of eating whatever he likes. Both wheat and rice can be given to the patient, but care should be taken to ensure that his stomach is not overloaded. Raw and bitter vegetables are always useful for such patients. The patient should be given fruits in adequate quantities. Leafy vegetables like fenugreek leaves, asafoetida, ginger, and garlic are extremely useful for these patients. The patients should avoid pickles, fried food and cool drinks.

Other regimens: The patient should use a mosquito net to save himself from the germ-carrying parasites thus preventing infection. Since the patient becomes weak, he should not exert himself or do any heavy exercise. He should take adequate rest but sleep during the daytime is prohibited.

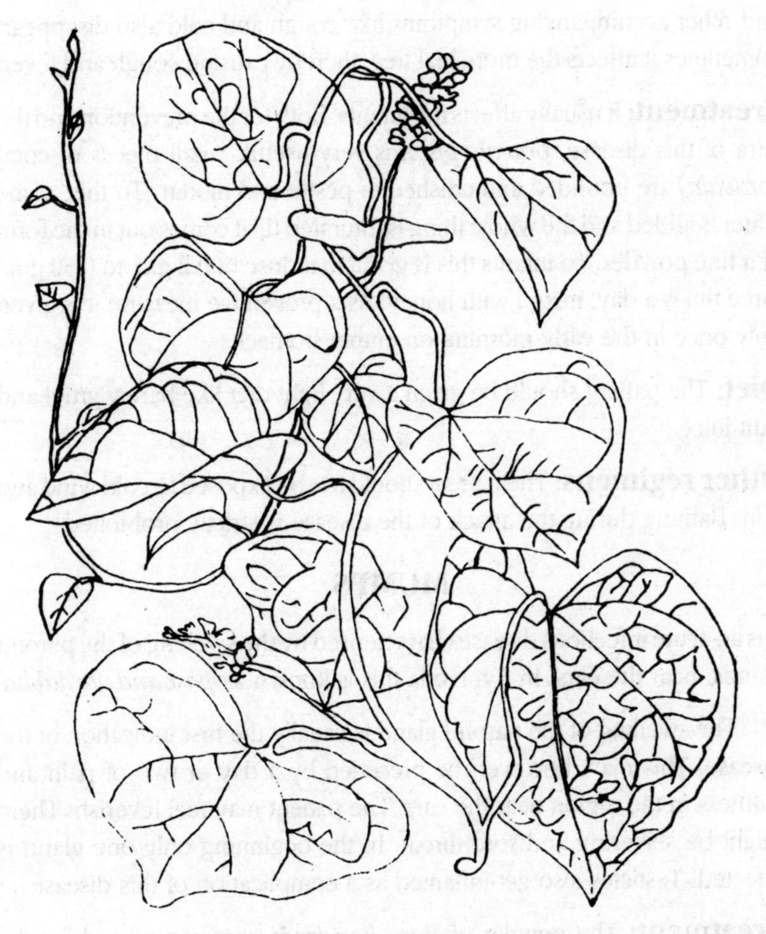

Fig. 2 *Tinospora cordifolia* (*guduchi*)

MEASLES

It is a highly infectious disease characterised by the catarrh of the respiratory passages and a widespread eruption on the skin. In Ayurveda this is known as *romantika.*

It usually occurs during spring and autumn seasons. In the beginning the patient gets cough, cold and fever. The eyes become red, followed by drowsiness, anorexia and even diarrhoea. Eruptions start from the forehead, and they are small and red. In about 3-4 days, this spreads all over the body. When the eruptions fully disappear, the fever comes down and other accompanying symptoms like cough and cold also disappear. Sometimes it affects the bronchial tree, thereby causing cough and fever.

Treatment: It usually affects the infants. Both for the prevention and the cure of this disease, *pravala pishti* is very useful. Small pieces of coral (*pravala)* are pounded and crushed in pestle and mortar. To this, some water is added and the whole thing is triturated till it comes out in the form of a fine powder. To infants this is given in a dose of 0.2 gm to 0.50 gm., three times a day, mixed with honey. As a preventive measure it is given only once in the early morning on empty stomach.

Diet: The patient should be given a very light diet like barley gruel and fruit juice.

Other regimens: The patient should not be exposed to cold wind and rain. Bathing during the attack of the disease is strictly prohibited.

MUMPS

It is an acute infectious disease characterised by the swelling of the parotid glands, near the ears. In Ayurveda this is known as *pashana gardabha.*

The swelling of the parotid gland is usually the first indication of the disease. This may, however, be preceded by a day or two of pain and stiffness in the region near the ears. The patient may feel feverish. There might be shivering and sore throat. In the beginning only one gland is affected. Testicles also get inflamed as a complication of this disease.

Treatment: The powder of *daru haridra* is commonly used for the treatment of this condition. The wood of this plant is made into a fine powder and mixed with honey and ghee. It is slightly warmed and applied over the affected part. This should be done preferably at bedtime. The affected areas should be given dry hot fomentation. Internally, *Naradiya Lakshmivilasa* should be given to the patient in a dose of two tablets three times a day, mixed with honey.

Diet: During the attack of this disease, the patient usually loses appetite. Only liquids should be given to the patient. He should avoid fried and sour things. Garlic, ginger, black pepper and long pepper are very useful in this condition.

Other regimens: The patient should avoid taking hot and solid food and should not expose himself to cold wind and rain. He should also keep a woollen scarf around his neck and head to keep them warm for an early recovery.

FILARIA

This is commonly caused by a parasite called *Filaria bancrofti.* Embryos of this parasite are carried from the patient to a healthy man by mosquitos. In Ayurveda, this condition is known as *shlipada*.

The early symptoms of this disease are urticaria, inflammation of the lymph glands as well as lymphatic channels, inflammation of the testicles and fever. The lymph glands become tender and the lymph channels become red. The fever usually starts with shivering and continues for one to three days. Usually the glands at the base of the thighs are primarily affected. Recurrent attacks of this fever, which is common, lead to hydrocele or elephantiasis. The skin of the swollen region of the leg slowly becomes thickened and rough. Subsequently, abscesses may appear and this may lead to ulceration. Warts may also appear over the skin and it becomes leathery. The weight of the enlarged scrotum and the swollen leg may at times cause impediment in the movements of the patient.

Treatment: This disease is commonly found in marshy areas where there is stagnant water. Drinking water from the wells and ponds and even from the tubewells of this area makes a person susceptible to the attacks of this parasite. It is, therefore, necessary that persons inhabiting such localities should drink boiled water. If dried ginger is added to the water before boiling, it serves as a very good preventive measure. To prevent mosquito bite, mosquito nets should be regularly used.

The leaves of *bel* tree are very useful in the treatment of this condition. Taking three *bel* leaves every day helps both in the prevention and cure of this condition. The drug popularly used for this disease is known as *Nityananda rasa*. It is to be given to the patient in a dose of 0.5 gm., two times a day, on empty stomach. Usually this medicine is in the form of tablets, each tablet weighing 0.5 gm. It is to be made into a powder in a porcelain mortar and mixed with honey before it is given to the patient. Adding juice of *bel* leaves to this medicine strengthens its action.

Nityananda rasa is very well tolerated during winter season. It produces a little heat for which a larger dose of it cannot be given to the patient during summer season. In winter and rainy seasons, the dose of the medicine can be increased. For this medicine to act on the body, it should be taken continuously for a period of two months. In acute conditions, where there is inflammation as well as redness and tenderness of the glands and lymph channels and also fever, this medicine acts immediately. But even if the symptoms are over, this has to be continued for a sufficiently long time to create an atmosphere in the body by which the filaria parasite will not be able to thrive.

To relieve pain, ulceration, oozing of water, etc., from the affected parts, *Malla sindura* is often used. This drug is available in the form of crystals because it is prepared by the process of sublimation. It is to be made into a fine powder by grinding in a porcelain mortar and given to the patient in a dose of 250 mg, twice a day. In summer season, the dose should be reduced to 125 mg, twice a day. It should be well mixed with honey and given to the patient. It contains arsenic along with other ingredients. But during processing, the adverse effect of arsenic gets neutralised and normally it does not produce any toxic effect even if taken for a prolonged period.

Diet: Sour and stale foods like curd and pickles should be avoided. The patient should take bitter things like bitter gourd, *neem* leaves and bitter variety of drumstick, green banana, *patola*, brinjals, cabbage and cauliflower. Garlic and ginger are very useful for such patients. About ten raw garlic cloves should be given to the patient every day if he can tolerate its smell. Otherwise, the garlic should be fried in butter or ghee and given to the patient. For drinking, water boiled with dried ginger should be used.

Other regimens: The patient should avoid residing in marshy areas. In rainy season, he should avoid exposing himself to rains. Both in winter and rainy seasons, he should take bath with hot water only, and as far as possible drink hot water.

CHAPTER 5

DISEASES OF RESPIRATORY SYSTEM

BRONCHIAL ASTHMA

ASTHMA IS of many types. The one commonly found is called bronchial asthma. In Ayurveda, this disease is known as *tamaka shvasa*. In Ayurveda it is considered to originate from the affliction of the stomach and other parts of gastro-intestinal tract. In most of the cases, therefore, either in the beginning of the disease or before each attack, the patient suffers from indigestion, constipation or even diarrhoea.

The seat of manifestation of the disease is lungs. Because of pressure, the heart also gets involved. Usually before the attacks, the patient gets nasal congestion, even obstruction and sneezing. In Ayurveda, therefore, both for the prevention and cure of this disease, primary attention is given to stomach, bowels, nose and lungs. Simultaneously, in chronic cases, care is taken to strengthen the heart.

Treatment: For this disease, the medicines commonly used in Ayurveda are *Chyavana prasha* and *Agastya rasayana*. Both these medicines are composed of many drugs. But the chief ingredient of *Chyavana prasha* is the fruit of *amalaki*. This is one of the important sources of Vitamin C. Ordinarily, Vitamin C is found in many citrus fruits. But they get destroyed when they are exposed to the heat of sun or fire. *Amalaki*, however, is an exception, and the Vitamin C content of it does not get destroyed even after boiling for considerable period.

The fruit of *haritaki* is the main ingredient of the other medicine, viz., *Agastya rasayana*. This is also known as *Agastya haritaki* in some classics.

Of these two, viz., *Chyavanaprasha* and *Agastya rasayana*; the former is used more as a tonic and is specifically indicated in the cases of bronchial asthma, where the patient is emaciated and weak. *Agastya rasayana* is given to patients of bronchial asthma who are constipated and also to those who often complain of sneezing, blocking of the nostrils and congestion of the throat.

Both these drugs are in the form of a linctus and can be taken in a dose of upto two teaspoonfuls three times a day. Care should be taken to see that the normal appetite of the patient is maintained. If taken in heavy doses, at times, there is suppression of appetite, and in that case the dose of the medicine should be reduced. *Agastya rasayana*, if taken in heavy dose, may cause loose motions and in that case the dose of the medicine should also be reduced.

Both these medicines are to be taken before food, preferably on empty stomach, and at bedtime. A cup of warm milk or even warm water should be given after these medicines. They are to be taken during and even after the attack of asthma. They have both preventive and curative value. It takes some time for the action of these medicines to be noticed. Even though they might give some relief immediately after their intake, they usually take two to three weeks to act fully. In chronic cases, they may take still more time. Therefore, one should not doubt their utility if the attack is not stopped immediately after their intake. But they will certainly reduce the acuteness of the attack immediately, and the duration of the attack will be comparatively shorter. Even the gap between two attacks will increase and the patient will have time to restore his health in order to successfully fight the next attack.

Along with this, *Sitopaladi churna* may be taken, three to four times a day, in one teaspoonful dose, mixed with honey. The powder if taken alone may cause a little irritation in the throat. Therefore, it should be thoroughly mixed with honey and made to a linctus consistency before intake. This makes the medicine palatable and easy to take. In the same manner, and same dose, *pippali* powder may be used.

There are many other medicines in Ayurveda, for the treatment of bronchial asthma. Some medicines containing mineral products are useful in reducing the attacks of asthma immediately. They are *Shvasa kasa chintamani rasa, Suvarna pushpasuga rasa, Kanakasava,* etc. These medicines may at times produce side effects. Therefore, they should preferably be taken under the supervision of an expert physician.

Diet: The patient should strictly avoid curd, butter-milk, banana, guava and fried things. At night, he should take light food and as far as possible should avoid all sour things. Dry grapes, pulses like *kulattha* are useful in this condition. Smoking should be avoided and intake of tea or coffee should be reduced to the minimum — not more than two cups in any case. Alcoholic beverages can be taken but only in small quantity. The patient should not expose himself to rain and severe cold-wind. He should not indulge in hard exercise.

BRONCHITIS

The disease bronchitis is characterised by the inflammation of the bronchi of the lungs which results in the discharge (coughing out) of a muco-purulent substance, commonly known as phlegm. It is of several types depending upon the nature of the discharge. Bronchitis can occur as a symptom of many other diseases like tuberculosis. In all such cases, one or the other type of germ is considered to be the causative factor.

In Ayurveda, this disease is called *kasa roga. Krimis* or germs are known in Ayurveda to cause the disease. But they are not considered to be the primary causative factors. Ayurveda considers *kasa roga* to be caused primarily by the impairment of digestion. For the treatment of bronchitis, therefore, drugs having properties to correct both the lungs and stomach are selected by ayurvedic physicians.

Treatment: Whatever the cause may be, the simplest treatment for bronchitis is to give to the patient one teaspoonful of *haridra* (turmeric) powder mixed with a cup of milk, two to three times a day, depending upon the severity of the condition. This acts better if given on an empty stomach. This is an absolutely harmless recipe which can be given to any patient irrespective of age, sex or condition of the disease.

The popular recipe, commonly used as a household remedy for this condition is the powder of *shunthi* (dried ginger), *pippali* (long pepper) and *maricha* (black pepper) - all three mixed in equal quantity. The mixture is given in a dose of half teaspoonful, three to four times a day, depending upon the severity of the disease. This powder can be added to tea or coffee, and taken. All these three medicines, taken together, are known in Ayurveda as *trikatu* or *tryushana*, and they are well known for their action on the lungs and stomach. They promote digestion and metabolism in the body and thus inhibit the production of the factors responsible for the causation of the infection and inflammation of the bronchi. Simultaneously they help in the expectoration of the accumulated phlegm, and make the breathing easy. At times, because of infection, the patient also suffers from fever and these medicines cure fever as well, because of their anti-pyretic and stimulant effects. These drugs create such an environment in the body, and specially in the lungs of the individual, that the harmful germs do not find it congenial to thrive, not to speak of their growth and multiplication.

All these three drugs are also used in the kitchen as spices; hence they have no harmful effect whatsoever on the body. If taken in excess they may produce a little burning sensation in the chest, and in that case, the dose should be reduced, or some more honey should be added to the powder, and then taken.

A medicinal plant called *vasa* is very useful in curing cough and bronchitis, specially when they become chronic. The juice of the leaves of this plant is generally used in a dose of two teaspoonful, three times a day. The taste of this juice is slightly bitter. Thus to make it palatable, an equal quantity of honey should be added. This plant naturally grows in almost all parts of India except in deserts and snow-clad mountains.

Bronchitis is often associated with congested throat. In that case, *khadiradi vati* should be kept in the mouth and sucked slowly. About five tablets can be used each day. This produces a soothing effect on the throat and relieves the congestion. The main ingredient of this drug is *khadira*.

Diet: Curd and other sour things should be avoided. Sour fruits, including banana and guava are also contra-indicated.

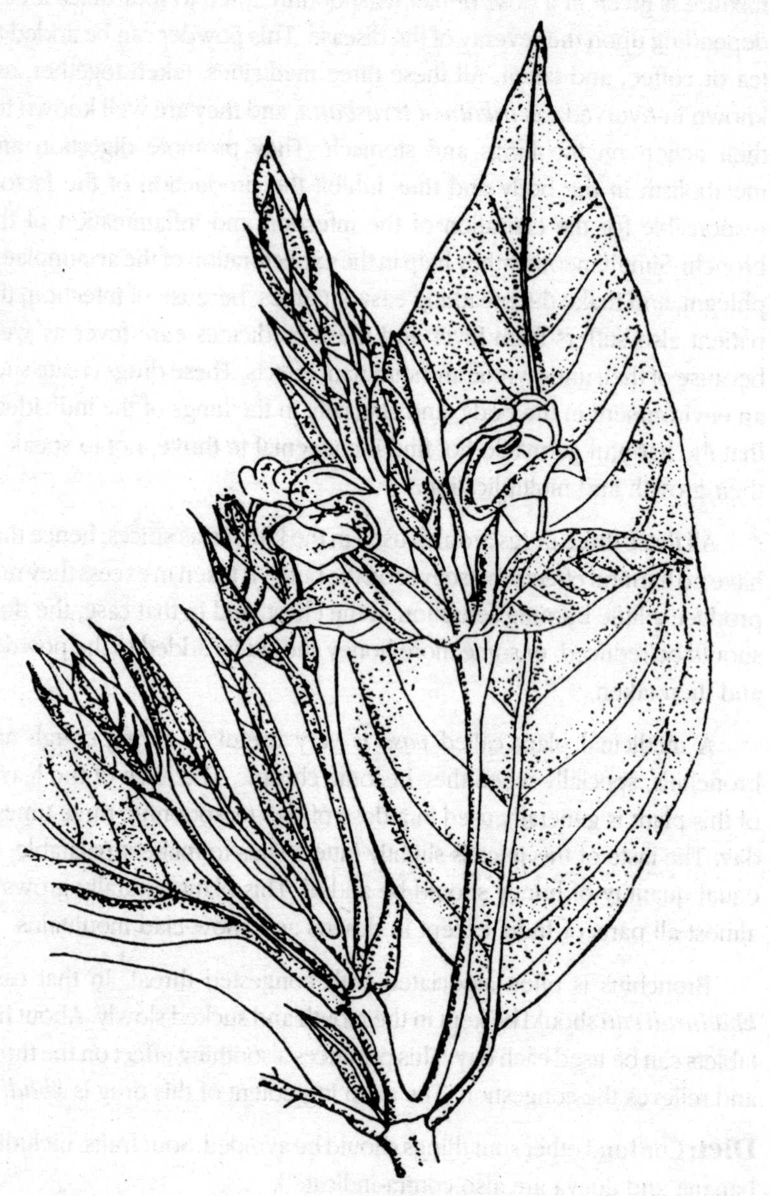

Fig. 3 *Adhatoda vasica* (*vasa*)

Other regimens: Exposure to cold wind and rain should be avoided. Bath in cold water (specially in winter) is contra-indicated, more so when bronchitis is in its acute phase.

HAEMOPTYSIS

Spitting of blood while coughing is called haemoptysis. This is primarily caused by such diseases as tuberculosis and cancer of the lungs. In Ayurveda it is included in the group of *urdhvaga rakta pitta*. The patient spits blood while coughing. Sometimes blood is accompanied with mucus.

Treatment: *Vasaka* is the drug of choice for the treatment of this condition. It is given to the patient in the form of juice in a dose of two teaspoonfuls four times a day. It is bitter in taste and is, therefore, given to the patient, mixed with honey.

Pravala pishti, a preparation of coral, is the drug of choice for the treatment of this condition. It is given in a dose of one gm. four times a day, mixed with honey.

Diet: Hot and spicy things should be avoided and the patient should be given pomegranate, *amalaki*, cow's milk and water. Old rice, soup of *patola, moong, masur* and meat can be given to the patient.

Other regimens: The patient should not do any exercise, and take complete rest. He should avoid the sun.

HICCUPS

Hiccups are characterised by the sharp inspiratory sound produced with the spasm of glottis and diaphragm. In Ayurveda it is known as *hikka roga*. Depending upon the *doshas* involved in the pathogenesis of the disease, different types of symptoms are manifested.

Treatment: The ash of peacock feather is considered to be the best therapy for the condition. It is given in a dose of 0.125 gm. six times a day, mixed with honey. *Eladi vati*, which contains cardamom as an important ingredient, is popularly given for the treatment of this condition. It is given with honey to be sucked in a dose of one tablet six times a day. For the alleviation of upward movement of *vayu*, *Sukumara ghrita* should be given to the patient in a dose of one teaspoonful three times a day with milk.

Diet: *Kulattha* is very useful in this condition. The juice, the soup or the *dal* preparation of this can be given to the patient. Old rice, *patola*, tender radish, lemon, goat's milk and garlic can also be given. Fatty food, heavy and cold food and *masha* are contra-indicated in this condition.

Other regimens: The patient should be given psycho-therapy if the hiccup is produced as a result of psychoneurotic conditions. The patient should be given rest and he should not suppress the natural urges in any form.

PLEURISY

The inflammation of the pleura which is the covering membrane over the lungs is known as pleurisy. It is normally classified into three categories, depending upon the effects produced by this inflammation. If this inflammatory process leads to fibrinose deposit it is described as dry pleurisy; if however, lot of fluid is exudated during the process of inflammation and gets deposited in the pleural cavity, then this condition is known as pleurisy with effusion. If however, there is pus formation then the condition is described as purulent pleurisy.

It is usually associated with pain in the chest during movement, coughing, difficulty in breathing and high temperature. The patient feels difficulty in lying down. In Ayurveda, this condition is called *parshva shula* and it is caused primarily by the aggravation of *vayu* and *kapha*.

Treatment : *Shringa bhasma* is considered to be specific for the treatment of pleurisy. It is the deer's horn which is cut into small pieces, processed, and burnt to ashes. This is made into a fine powder and then used in medicine. Half a gm. of this is to be given to the patient, three or four times a day, depending upon the acuteness and seriousness of the condition. This is to be mixed with honey and given to the patient.

If there is pleurisy with infusion, then 0.250 gm. of *Naradiya Lakshmivilas* should be added to this powder and taken four times a day. If there is cough and phlegm, then to the two medicines mentioned above,

0.125 gm. of *Rasa sindoora* should be added to each one of these doses. *Rasa sindoora* is prepared by specially processing mercury and sulphur over fire. Care should be taken not to use this medicine for a long time. As soon as cough and pain subside, this medicine should be withdrawn and the remaining two should be continued.

If there is pus formation in this fluid and if as a consequence, the patient is suffering from fever, then it is always better to add 0.125 gm. of *Suvarna vasanta malati* and the whole thing given to the patient four times a day, mixed with honey.

Diet: The patient is strictly prohibited from taking any fried stuff. He should also not take iced food. Bitter gourd, *patola,* brinjal, lady's finger, cauliflower, cabbage and potato can be given to the patient. The patient loses his appetite normally and then he gets constipation. If it is there, then efforts should be made to relieve the patient of constipation. This will give lot of comfort to the patient.

Other regimens: The patient should refrain from any physical exercise, sex indulgence, exposure to cold wind or rain. Bed rest is essential for such type of patients; but during winter season, he should not be permitted to sleep during daytime.

TUBERCULOSIS

Tuberculosis is caused by *Tubercular bacilli.* It primarily affects the lungs. Other organs like the bones, lymph glands and intestines are also affected by the disease. In Ayurveda this disease is known as *rajayakshma* which literally means the kind of diseases.

In Ayurveda, bacilli are considered to be the causative agents of this disease. They are, however, considered as secondary factors for its causation. The primary factor is the imbalance of the *doshas* and vitiation of the tissue elements in the body. Tubercular bacilli are present in the throats of many individuals. They do not all suffer from this disease. As a seed lies dormant without germination in a barren land, similarly tubercular bacilli do not manifest the disease unless the *doshas* in the body are simultaneously vitiated. For the vitiation of *doshas* the following four factors are considered to be very important from Ayurvedic point of view:

(a) irregularity in the intake of food;

(b) performance of exercise or hard labour in excess of one's capacity;

(c) suppression of natural urges; and

(d) excessive sexual indulgence.

The patient suffering from tuberculosis loses weight rapidly and gets fever and cough. There is also hoarseness of voice, loss of appetite, pain in chest, spitting of mucus containing blood, headache, bodyache and weakness. The patient experiences burning sensation in the soles of the feet and palms. This disease is often characterised by night sweating.

Treatment: *Vasa* is commonly used by Ayurvedic physicians for the treatment of this disease. The juice from the leaves of this drug is given in a dose of 30 ml. four times a day, mixed with honey. It reduces the cough, helps in expectoration and cures the burning sensation.

Naradiya mahalakshmi vilasa which contains, among other things, gold, is the drug of choice for the treatment of this diseases. This is to be given in the dose of 0.200 gm. three times a day, with honey. This works exceedingly well when the patient suffers from chronic bronchitis and cold. When there is excessive fever, night sweating and a burning sensation in the palms and on the soles of the feet, *Svarna vasanta malati* is the drug of choice. It contains, among other things, pearls and gold.

Lasuna or garlic is a very useful medicine for the treatment of this disease. 30 gm. of garlic are to be boiled in about 500 ml. of milk and $^1/_2$ ltr. of water. After boiling, it is reduced to one-fourth and filtered. This medicated milk may be given to the patient twice daily.

To improve the digestion of the patient, he should be given 30 ml. of *Drakshasava* after food with an equal quantity of water. *Chyavana prasha* is also given to the patient suffering from tuberculosis. It contains *amalaki* as one of its important ingredients. This is exceedingly nourishing and useful in all types of diseases of the chest. It is given in a dose of two teaspoonfuls two times a day on an empty stomach with milk. As the

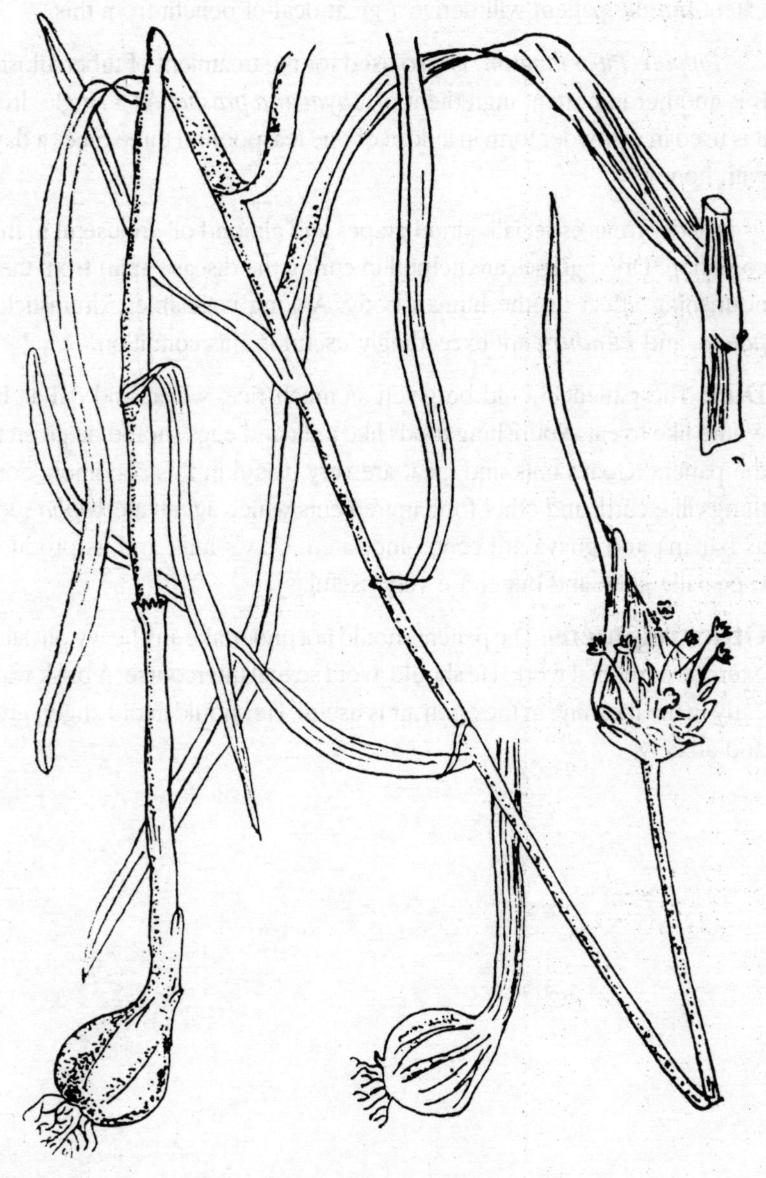

Fig. 4 *Allium sativum* (*rasona/lasuna*)

digestive power of the patient improves, he should be given this medicine in a larger quantity. This is more a food than a medicine and as much as 50 to 100 gm. a day can be given. This may suppress the appetite to some extent but the patient will derive a great deal of benefit from this.

Pippali (Piper longum) is also used for the treatment of tuberculosis. It is another important ingredient of *Chyavana prasha.* As a single drug it is used in a powder form in a dose of one teaspoonful three times a day, with honey.

All dry fruits especially dried grapes and almond oil are useful in this condition. Dried grapes are helpful in curing the disease apart from their nourishing effect on the human body. Among vegetables, drumsticks, *patola,* and *kunduru* are exceedingly useful in this condition.

Diet: The patient should be given as much rice, wheat and dal as he would like to eat. Nourishing foods like milk and eggs should be given to the patient. Goat's milk and meat are very useful in this condition. Sour things like curd, and other food ingredients which aggravate *kapha* such as banana and guava are contra-indicated. Cow's milk and its products especially ghee and butter are very useful.

Other regimens: The patient should not undertake any heavy physical exercise or mental work. He should avoid sexual intercourse. A brisk walk early in the morning in the open air is useful. He should avoid anger, grief and anxiety.

CHAPTER 6

DISEASES OF SKIN AND HAIR

BALDNESS

BALDNESS MAY be local or general. Normally, people are found with hairlessness on a circumscribed area of the skull or the beard. In worst cases, hair of the beard, eye lashes, eyebrows, armpits and even pubic region is lost. In Ayurveda this condition is known as *khalitya.*

Excessive mental worry, anxiety and anger are considered to be the cause of this ailment. A type of pathogenic organism is also considered to be the cause of loss of hair from the body including the head.

Even though it does not cause any physical pain, it creates a lot of psychic problems. A sort of inferiority complex develops in the mind of the patient, specially because of the effect on baldness on beauty.

Treatment: *Bhringaraja* is the drug of choice for the treatment of the disease. *Maha bhringaraja taila* or *Nilibhringadi taila* is commonly prescribed by the physicians. This is to be gently massaged over the scalp about one hour before taking bath. By this massage some of the existing weak hair fall out. Therefore, in the beginning, the hair will look thinner and the baldness would appear as if increasing. The patient should not get scared by this. In fact, it is better if the whole head is thoroughly shaved and then this oil is used for massage. It should be used constantly for about six months before any significant results could be achieved. Powder of *bhringaraja* should be give to the patient orally. One teaspoonful of this powder should be mixed with honey and given on empty stomach, twice a day.

Elephant tusk is very popularly used by Ayurvedic physicians for the treatment of this ailment. The tusk is cut into small pieces and burnt to ashes. This is rubbed with ghee or honey over the patches, daily. This can preferably be done at night so that the ash or *bhasma* of elephant tusk remains in contact with the skin of the skull overnight.

Some irritating medicines are also used for the treatment of this condition. They work very well if baldness appears in young age. *Ashvakanchuki rasa* is used by Ayurvedic physicians for this purpose. It is basically a strong purgative. These tablets are crushed, mixed with honey and externally applied. This is applied over the skull in the afternoon and allowed to dry up. The patient should go to bed without washing his head. In the beginning, application of this medicine causes a little redness and irritation in the skull but slowly hair begin to grow.

Diet: Weakness is often the cause of hair fall and the patient should, therefore, take nourishing diet. Meat, fish, ghee, butter, milk and such other high-protein diet is normally recommended. Care should be taken to keep the liver free from overwork. Therefore, fried things are strictly prohibited for such patients.

Other regimens: Worry is one of the primary causes of baldness. The patient should, therefore, try to maintain a tranquil disposition and avoid anxiety. Spending sleepless nights, excessive sexual indulgence, and suppression of the natural urges of stool and urine, are strictly prohibited. A constipated patient is likely to get disturbed sleep. The tension further aggravates the baldness. The patient should, therefore, see that he gets clear motions every day. A glass of water early morning will be quite helpful for the patient. It will be necessary for him to walk for about 2-3 kilometres either in the morning or in the evening.

Many hair oils are advertised in newspapers to cure baldness. Most of them make exaggerated claims. The patient is, therefore, advised not to go in for them but consult a physician.

ECZEMA

Eczema means a "boiling over" of the skin and is characterised by spontaneous eruptions. It is also characterised clinically by papulo-vesiculated eruptions. In Ayurveda it is called *vicharchika*. It is primarily of two types, the dry and the wet. In the former, there is no exudation whereas in the latter type water may come out of the patches, either by scratching or without it.

Treatment: The eczema affected patch should be cleaned daily with warm water boiled with the bark of the neem tree. After cleaning, the paste of the bark of the neem tree should be applied over it and allowed to dry. *Paradadi malham* is very commonly used by Ayurvedic physicians for the treatment of this condition. It contains, among others, mercury and sulphur and it should be applied three times daily. For internal administration, *Shuddha gandhaka* should be given to the patient in a dose of 0.200 gm, twice a day, mixed with honey, on empty stomach. In chronic and obstinate cases, *Rasa manikya* can also be given. It is an arsenic preparation and should be given with proper care. Normally, it is given in a dose of 0.125 gm., twice a day, mixed with honey. It is available in a scale form and in small pieces. This should be administered after making it into a fine powder.

In case of eczema of infants, both *Paradadi malham* and *Rasa manikya* should not be used. They are poisonous and may cause other complications. For external application, *Guduchyadi taila* or *Brihat marichyadi taila* should be used.

The patient should not be constipated and if so, he should be given one teaspoonful of *triphala* powder at bedtime regularly.

Diet: Salt intake should be reduced. It is necessary specially if the patient is given *Rasa manikya* internally. Sour things including pickles and curd are strictly prohibited. Bitter things like bitter gourd, bitter variety of drumstick and neem flowers are very useful for these patients. Turmeric is exceedingly useful for the patients having this disease. It can be applied externally over the eczematous patch and it can be taken internally along with milk in a dose of one teaspoonful, twice a day.

Other regimens: Certain types of garments interfere with the evaporation of the sweat. Nylons, terylenes and other synthetic fibres should, therefore, be avoided. The patient should use as little cloth as possible. The eczematous patches particularly should be kept free from any tight clothing.

GREYING OF HAIR

Greying of hair is generally considered as a sign of old age. At times, greying starts even at a young age. This is considered as a morbidity. In Ayurveda this is called *palitya.*

According to Ayurveda excessive passion, anger and psychic strain results in greying of hair. Persons with *paittika* type of constitution are prone to be affected by this ailment. Persons suffering from chronic cold and sinusitis and those who use warm water for washing their hair are more likely to be victims of this condition.

Treatment: *Bhringaraja* and *amalaki* are popularly used for the treatment of this condition. Medicated oil prepared by boiling these two drugs, viz., *Maha Bhringaraja taila* is used externally for massaging the head. The powder of these two drugs is also used internally in a dose of one teaspoonful three times daily with milk. The oil prepared from the seeds of the neem tree is used for inhalation twice a day for about a month. Along with this, the patient should be advised to take only milk as his diet.

Another drug popularly used for this condition is *bhallataka.* This has a slightly allergic effect. Therefore, it has to be processed carefully before use. Normally this is given to the patient in the form of a linctus in a dose of one teaspoonful twice daily followed by milk.

Diet: These therapies will be effective only when the patient observes diet restrictions. As far as possible, he should take only milk and sugar. Salt should be avoided. Sour things like curd are not useful. Pungent, hot and spicy food should be avoided.

Other regimens: The patient should not remain awake for a long time at night and should be kept free from worry, anxiety and passion. If suffering from cold and sinusitis, prompt and careful treatment should be given. Hot water should never be used for washing the hair. Cold water should always be used for bathing.

LEUCODERMA

This disease is characterised by localised loss of pigmentation of the skin.

According to Ayurveda this is caused by some morbidity in the liver which results in the deficient production of *pitta*. These white patches of leucoderma often go without any physical trouble. It, however, creates a great deal of worry to the patient suffering from it because it disfigures him. This disease is also hereditary. Therefore, the marriage of the children of the patient, suffering from this disease, becomes a problem. There is a social stigma against this disease. In Ayurveda, this is considered to be a type of *kushtha*. Common men who are ignorant of the actual implications of these technical terms consider leucoderma to be a type of leprosy and thus, shun the patient. This is the result of a misunderstanding. Actually in Ayurveda the term *kushtha* means any obstinate skin disease including leprosy. Because leucoderma is one of the obstinate skin diseases it is included under *kushtha* and it has nothing to do with leprosy in any form.

At times these skin patches become reddish brown, and small eruptions appear over them. They cause considerable amount of itching which is followed by watery exudation and burning sensation.

According to Ayurveda leucoderma appearing in the joint of skin and mucous membrane is difficult to cure. This disease is also difficult to be treated when it appears in old persons.

Treatment: Leucoderma is often caused by some disturbance in digestion. People suffering from chronic dysentery are more prone to be affected by this disease. Therefore, in the first instance steps are taken to correct the digestion and dysentery, if any, in the patient. *Kutaja* is the drug of choice in this condition. The bark of this plant is used in the form of a powder in the dose of one teaspoonful three times a day. Some other carminatives and laxatives can be given to the patient in a dose of four tablets three times (12 tablets in total) a day. The most important ingredient of this recipe is *katuki*. This drug stimulates the liver and corrects its impairment which helps in the cure of leucoderma. It also contains copper in the form of *bhasma*. This metal helps in the metabolism and synthesis of melanin pigments.

The other drug which is commonly used for the treatment of this disease is *bhallataka*. It is prepared in the form of a linctus by adding some other medicines. This is given to the patient in a dose of one teaspoonful

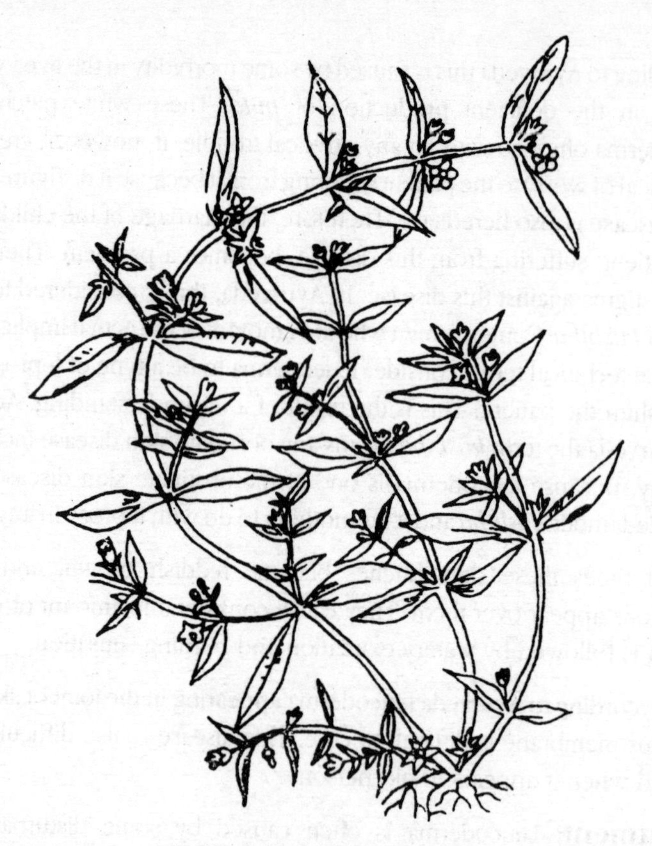

Fig. 5 *Eclipta alba* (*bhringaraja*)

twice a day. This medicine may have some adverse effects on the body. These effects can, however, be prevented by taking suitable action well in advance. Before taking this linctus the inner mucous membrane should be covered with a coating of ghee or butter. Care should be taken so that the linctus does not come into direct contact with the mucous membrane. Immediately after taking this medicine some milk may be given to the patient. While taking this medicine the patient should avoid hot things and should not expose himself to heat or sun rays. If in spite of all these precautions skin rashes appear, then the pulp of raw coconut should be given to the patient to be eaten. This eliminates all the toxic manifestations of the drug.

Bakuci is very popularly used for the treatment of this disease both in Ayurveda and allopathy. A paste prepared from the seeds of this drug is applied externally. The powder of this drug mixed with the decoction of *khadira and amalaki* is given to the patient in a dose of 1/2 teaspoon twice daily. The oil prepared by boiling *gunja* is also advisable for the treatment of leucoderma.

Diet: The patient should not be given salt in any form. The more he avoids salt the quicker will be the action of the drug. If found essential, rock-salt can be given in a small quantity only. Spices and other pungent things should be avoided. Vegetables having bitter taste like bitter gourd and bitter variety of drumstick are useful.

Other regimens: The patient should not expose himself to heat or sun in excess. Psychic factors are known to be responsible for precipitation and aggravation of this disease. The patient should, therefore, try to keep himself free from worry, anxiety and other forms of mental strain. Remaining awake at night for long should be avoided. Medicines suggested work better if the patient is free from constipation.

PRICKLY HEAT

It is an acute form of heat rash associated with excessive sweating, specially during humid climate. In Ayurveda this is known as a type of *pidaka*.

It consists of small superficial eruptions which look like grains of sand. It affects almost any part of the body. Pricking, burning sensation and itching cause a lot of discomfort, and may cause secondary bacterial infection.

Treatment: Persons having *paittika* type of physical constitution are more prone to get this skin trouble. As far as possible, such patients should avoid heat and humidity. Intake of *Pravala pishti* in a dose of 0.5 gms. twice a day, with honey, helps both in preventing and curing this disease.

Diet: Almond and almond oil, grapes, specially dry grapes, are very useful for these patients. Fruit juice should be given to them in plenty.

Other regimens: Use of fresh air and physical exercise helps both in preventing and curing this condition. Care should be taken to see that the sweat is wiped off the body as soon as it appears.

PSORIASIS

It is a chronic recurrent papulo-squamous skin disease with silvery grey scaling papules or flakes. Although the condition may occur on any part of the body, the most common sites are surfaces over the knees and elbows. In Ayurveda it is known as *eka-kushtha.* Blood impurities associated with some emotional factors are mentioned in Ayurveda as causes of this disease.

Since there is severe irritation on these patches the patient is unable to resist scratching. By scratching, scales come out of these patches and a shiny silver skin is exposed below the scales which is the characteristic feature of this disease. At times, because of violent itching, watery exudation and blood come out of these patches which produce a burning sensation.

Treatment: *Kushtha rakshasa taila* is highly efficacious in the treatment of this condition. It is rubbed externally over these patches and nearby areas especially when the patient feels like scratching. *Guggulu tiktaka ghrita* is given to the patients. It contains, among others, *guggulu* and five bitter drugs. It keeps the bowels clean, promotes digestion, stimulates the liver, purifies the blood and produces unctuousness in the body. It is to be started in a dose of one teaspoonful twice daily on an empty stomach, mixed with a cup of warm milk. The dose is to be gradually increased to six teaspoonfuls of the ghee twice daily or till the signs of proper unctuousness appear in the body of the patient. This is a preparatory treatment, and is usually given to the patient before the administration of the actual therapy. *Chanda maruta* is another medicine found useful for the treatment of this condition. Among others, it contains mercury and arsenic. It is usually given in a dose of 125 mg. twice daily mixed with honey on an empty stomach. Since some of the ingredients of drug are highly toxic, proper care should be taken during its administration.

Diet: Hot and spicy things should be avoided. The patient should avoid salt and curd. If at all found essential, rock-salt in small doses can be taken. All vegetables having bitter taste like bitter gourd, bitter variety of drumstick and flowers of neem tree are very useful in this condition.

Other regimens: The patient should avoid nylon and other synthetic fabrics. He should not use his nails for scratching the patches. Whenever itching sensation is there, the patient should be advised to rub *Kushtha rakshasa taila* over the patches.

RING WORM

This is a skin disease caused by fungi. In Ayurveda this is called *dadru*. The infection spreads peripherally and heals centrally with the result that the earlier region becomes a ring with scaly or vesicular border and a central zone of normal or recovered skin.

Treatment: The patient should take regular bath and wear clean and dry clothes. Bath with hot water boiled with neem leaves is extremely useful in this condition. Applying a paste of neem leaves over the affected areas of the skin is desirable. In chronic patients, application of *Paradadi malham* or *Dadrughna lepa* proves very useful. A drug called *Edgaja* is commonly used for the treatment. The seeds of this plant are taken in powder form and applied over the affected area in the form of a paste. Giving the patient *Shuddha gandhaka* internally proves very useful. It should be given in a dose of 0.2 gm., twice daily, mixed with honey. These medicines both internally and externally should be continued for some time, even after the patch is cured. There is every likelihood of the recurrence of this disease. Therefore, medicines should be continued for about 7 days after the patches have disappeared.

Diet: Sour things, including curd and pickles, should be avoided.

Other regimens: The patient should wear clean clothes and take bath daily with water boiled with *neem* leaves.

SCABIES

Scabies is a parasitic infestation and it usually spreads by physical contact. In Ayurveda it is known as *kachchhu*.

Usually, scabies affects the thin skin areas below the collar line. Thus, the interior auxiliary folds inside of the elbows, the ulnar side of the wrist joints and hands and the clefts of the fingers are the sites commonly affected on the upper limb. On the trunk the sites most commonly affected are female breasts, the abdomen, the male genital organ and buttocks. In the lower limb, the thigh, ankles and feet are generally affected. There are itching papules and it may be marked by scratching, inflammation, pus formation and eczema.

Treatment: Purified sulphur is commonly used in the treatment of scabies. About two gm. of raw sulphur is taken in a big spoon and to this, some cow's ghee is added so that the sulphur powder gets fully submerged in the ghee. The kitchen spoon is then kept over an oven and heated. As the ghee starts boiling the sulphur melts and gets mixed up with the ghee. In another pot cow's milk is kept and its mouth is covered with a thin cloth. Over this cloth, the hot ghee containing sulphur is poured and through this cloth, the sulphur comes down to the milk inside the pot. Coming in contact with milk, the sulphur gets solidified and it is to be taken out from the milk and washed with warm water. This process is to be repeated for seven times. The sulphur thereby not only becomes free from extraneous impurities, but also becomes non-toxic and therapeutically more effective when taken internally. This sulphur is to be made into a powder and kept in a dry bottle. This is to be given to the patient in a dose of 0.2 gm, two times per day, mixed with honey on empty stomach. The ghee which comes out of the milk to which sulphur is added is very useful for external application. This type of sulphur is well tolerated even by infants.

Care should be taken to see that the patient gets clean motion. If not, a laxative may be given to him.

The parts of the body affected by scabies should be washed daily with water boiled with neem leaves. Soap prepared with neem oil is very useful. Neem leaves can be chewed and taken internally also. Tender *neem* leaves which are not very bitter, are made into a pill of the size of a pea and given to the patient, twice a day.

Diet: Sweet and sour things should not be taken by the patient. Pickles, curd and molasses are strictly prohibited.

Other regimens: The patient should develop clean habits. He should take bath daily, if possible with water boiled with neem leaves. Exercises, brisk walk in fresh air in the morning and evening, are very useful for the patient.

URTICARIA

This is a vascular reaction of the skin characterised by the transient appearance of elevated patches which are redder or paler than the surrounding skin and often attended by itching. In Ayurveda this is called *shita pitta*.

Allergens, taking cold bath immediately after exercise, when the body is hot, and mental excitement are the most important factors for the causation of this disease. Intestinal worms and exposure to the cold wind often cause urticaria. These patches appear all over the body suddenly or gradually. There may be severe itching. The patient is usually constipated. He may get attacks of cold, cough, bronchitis and stomach disorder.

Treatment: *Haridra* is one of the popular household remedies. This is normally used in curry. a little excessive use of this in vegetables both prevents and cures urticaria. In the form of a paste by triturating its powder with water, it is given to the patient in a dose of two teaspoonfuls three times a day. It has a slightly bitter taste. So if the crude powder is disliked by the patient, it could be given by mixing with milk and sugar. A palatable preparation of *haridra* is known as *Haridra khanda.* It is available in the form of granules and can be given to the patient in a dose of one teaspoonful three times a day followed by a cup of warm water.

Gairika (red ochre) is also popularly used in this condition. After processing, it is given in a dose of one teaspoonful three times a day mixed with honey. *Kamadugha rasa,* which contains *gairika* in a significantly large quantity, is also given to the patient in a dose of 0.5 gm. four times a day with honey.

During an acute attack of this disease, *Suta shekhara rasa* and *Arogya vardhini rasa* can be given to the patient. Both these medicines either individually or in a compound form are given in a dose of 0.5 gm. three times a day, mixed with honey.

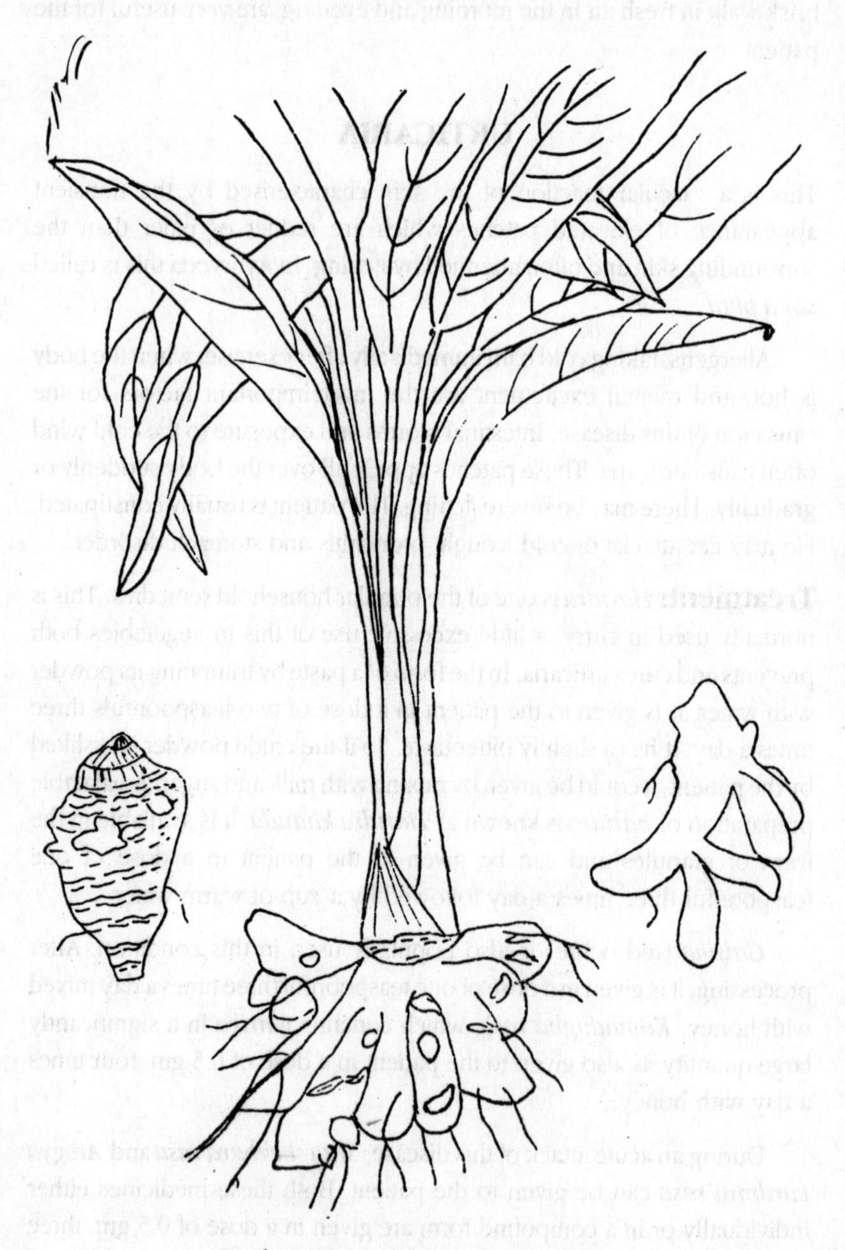

Fig. 6 *Curcuma longa* (*haridra or rajani*)

If the patient is constipated, he may be given the powder of *haritaki* in a dose of two teaspoonfuls at bedtime with hot water.

Diet: The patient should be given salt-free diet as far as possible. Sour things, like curd, are prohibited. All vegetables having bitter taste like bitter gourd and bitter variety of drumstick are useful in this condition. Onion and garlic can be given to the patient in good quantity.

Other regimens: During acute attacks of urticaria, the patient should be rubbed with mustard oil mixed with the powder of rock-salt. Thereafter, the whole body should be exposed to the sun and gently rubbed with a copper coin. This gives instant relief. If there are worms in the intestine, then they should be treated. Otherwise urticaria will appear again and again.

CHAPTER 7

DISEASES OF BLOOD AND CARDIO-VASCULAR SYSTEM

ANAEMIA

IN AYURVEDA, anaemia is known as *pandu.* The term anaemia means lack of red blood corpuscles or of haemoglobin. It may be caused by (1) haemorrhages from the body by injury, bleeding piles, or bleeding from nose, mouth, lungs, anus, genital tract, etc., (2) inadequate supply of blood-forming ingredients through food, (3) destruction of the blood corpuscles inside the body after they are formed, and (4) deficiency in the production of blood because of defective functioning of some organs of the body like stomach, liver and bone-marrow.

Oxygen is very important for the maintenance and functioning of body cells, and this oxygen is carried from the lungs to different parts of the body through the red blood corpuscles. When blood is deficient, the patient suffers from weakness even after a little work and there is evident paleness in the face as well as other parts of the body.

Treatment: There are different causes for bleeding from different parts of the body, and if the anaemia is due to any one of these, then the cause of the bleeding is to be treated first. For nutritional deficiency, food ingredients containing iron are to be taken. If the *pandu roga* is caused by the malfunction of any of the organs or viscera of the body like liver, stomach and bone-marrow, then the medicine commonly used by expert Ayurvedic physicians is *Punarnavadi mandura* or *Punarnava mandura* which contains about 22 ingredients. The most important ingredient of this formula is *mandura* which is a by-product of iron-ore and is considered to be rich in an assimilable form of iron. Various pharmaceutical processes have been prescribed for preparing it in powder or *bhasma* form and also to make it more assimilable.

Punarnava, the next important drug in this formula, possesses• rejuvenating properties. The viscera or part thereof, the vitiation of which produces anaemia, gets rejuvenated by the use of this drug. Other drugs included in this formula also stimulate the affected organs and regulate their functions. Some of them increase the appetite of the patient, and thus, food is properly digested, absorbed and assimilated. This medicine has no toxicity, it can be given even to a healthy man, and it will serve as an elixir.

Normally one gm. of this drug is given four times a day. This should be well mixed with honey or any other suitable syrup and made to the consistency of a linctus and taken. For children, the dose may be proportionately reduced.

Diet: In *pandu roga*, sour things specially curd, and fried things, which come in the way of the normal functioning of the liver, are prohibited. Green vegetables are considered to be useful. Sweets prepared by adding *til* seeds in a syrup prepared of *gur* (sugar candy) is considered to be very useful. This is specifically given when the liver function is affected. The outer husk of *til* seed contains a lot of iron, and therefore, it should not be removed while preparing sweets.

Other regimens: *Pandu roga*, according to Ayurveda, is considered to be caused by the vitiation of *pitta*. Purgation is considered to be the best therapy for correcting *pitta*. Therefore, while treating a case, constipation is corrected in the first instance. In a constipated patient, the medicines mentioned above do not work well. *Punarnava mandura*, itself, works as a mild laxative when administered in a large dose. But if the patient remains constipated even thereafter, *triphala* water is prescribed to be taken every day in the morning, on an empty stomach.

Apart from the medicine described above, there are many other medicines mentioned in Ayurveda, which are to be given in specific types of anaemia. Some of these medicines may become a little toxic if not used in the proper dose. In serious cases of anaemia, these drugs are to be used under the proper supervision of an Ayurvedic physician.

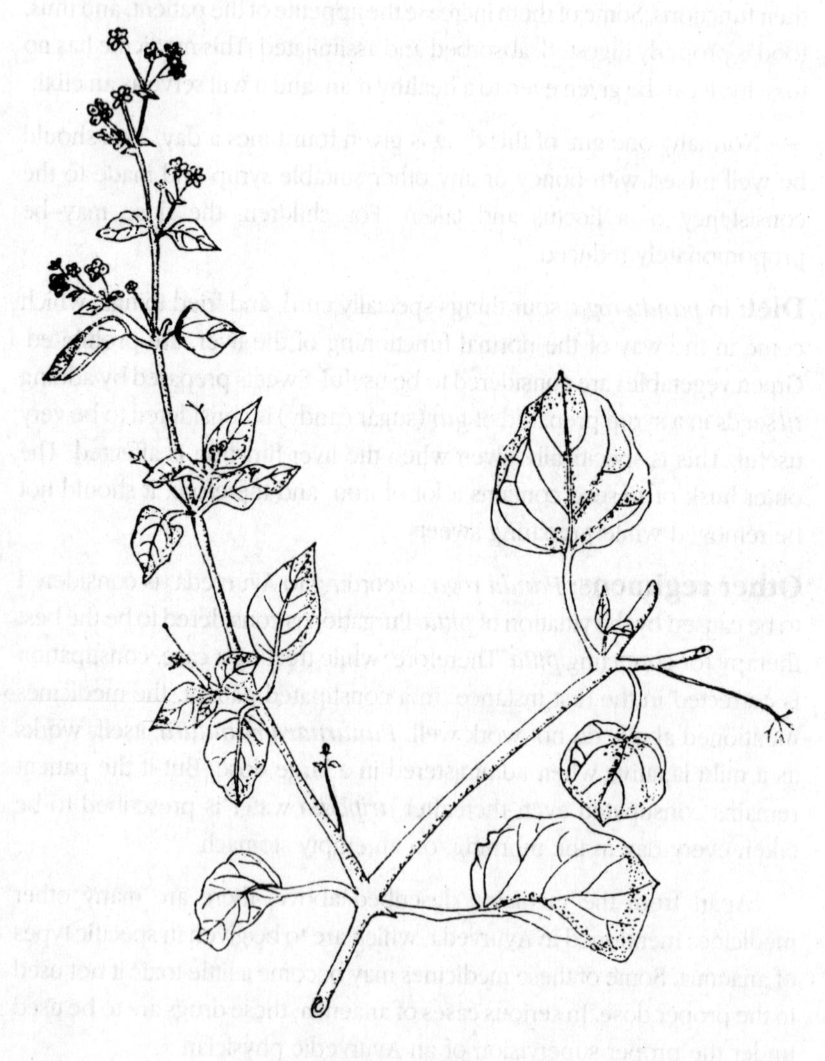

Fig. 7 *Boerhaavia diffusa* (*punarnava*)

HEART DISEASE

It is essentially a clinical syndrome of characteristic chest pain produced by increased work of the heart. It is usually relieved by rest. In most cases, it is manifested in front of the chest and mostly over the sternum. It may spread towards the left or right side of the chest. The pain radiates towards the left side very often. It may spread to the arms, neck, jaws and even the upper part of the abdomen. The left shoulder and the left arm are very often affected. The common man calls it heart disease. In Ayurveda it is known as *hridroga*. It is of several types depending upon the characteristic features of the pain. If the pain is acute, and of shifting nature, this is usually known as *vatika hridroga*. If it is associated with burning sensation, then it is called *paittika hridroga*. In *kaphaja hridroga*, the pain is usually very mild and it is associated with heaviness, nausea and cough.

It is caused by the obstruction to the coronary arteries. These are the blood vessels which travel through the wall of the heart and nourish the heart muscle. Since the heart muscle spends a huge amount of energy, it needs ceaseless nourishment. It naturally demands a good supply of blood. Any impairment of these blood vessels interferes with adequate blood flow to the heart muscles. If this blood flow is significantly diminished then the heart signals its difficulties by registering pain or discomfort in the chest.

Treatment: *Arjuna* is the drug of choice for the treatment of this disease. This is a big tree and its bark is used as medicine. The powder or decoction of its bark is given to the patient during and even after the attack. The powder is given to the patient in a dose of 1 gm., four times a day. If the heart disease is of *vatika* type, it is mixed with ghee. If it is of *paittika* type, then milk is used. In *kaphaja* type of heart disease it is mixed with honey or *pippali* powder. For decoction usually 30 gm. of the raw powder of the bark of the drug is boiled with approximately 500 ml. of water and reduced to one-fourth. This is then filtered, honey or ghee is added to it, and given to the patient. With honey, the decoction should become cold before mixing. Ghee is mixed, when the decoction is warm, and is given to the patient as such. There are many preparations of this drug, *arjuna*. *Arjunarishta* is commonly used by physicians. Six teaspoonfuls of this

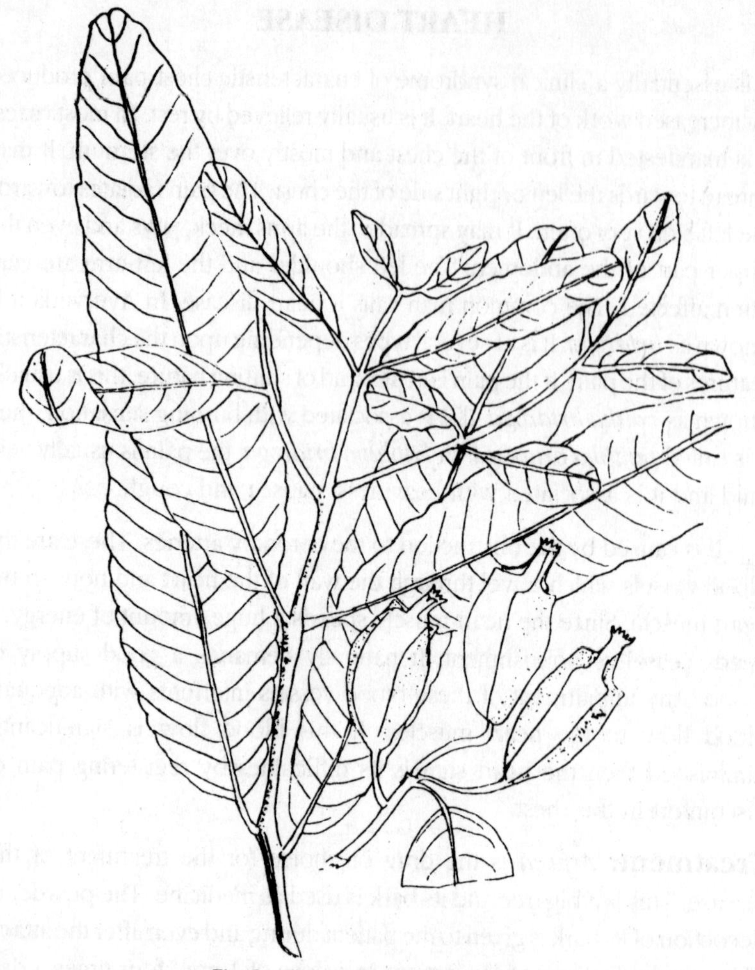

Fig. 8 *Terminalia arjuna* (*arjuna*)

liquid drug are given to the patient twice daily after food with an equal quantity of water. *Arujna* is boiled in cow's ghee, and this medicated ghee is given to the patients in a dose of 1 teaspoonful twice daily on empty stomach, mixed with a cup of warm milk. This preparation is known as *Arjuna ghrita.* This medicine should not be given to a person having a fat body. This is likely to add to his fat and may create more problems.

Other medicines used for different types of heart diseases are *Hridayarnava rasa* and *Prabhakara vati.* These medicines are available in the form of tablets. Two tablets are given to the patient, three or four times a day, depending on the seriousness of the disease.

At the time of acute attacks, *Mrigamadasava* is the ideal drug. It is a liquid medicine and given to the patient in a dose of 1/2 to 1 teaspoonful mixed with equal quantity of water. These medicines are to be used even after the attack has subsided. On exertion the patient may get the attack any time. It is, therefore, necessary for the patient to use the medicines mentioned above for about 6 months continuously.

Diet: Fried things, pulses and their preparations, and groundnut oil are prohibited. Ayurvedic physicians allow butter or ghee, and not groundnut oil. Cow's ghee, cow's milk and cow's butter are useful for the patient. Buffalo ghee and buffalo milk are not recommended. Stimulants like tea, coffee and alcoholic drinks are very harmful for such patients.

Other regimens: Ayurveda considers the functions of heart and mind interlinked. Disturbance in one affects the other. Therefore, patients having heart disease are advised by the Ayurvedic physicians to refrain from anxiety, worry, excessive sexual intercourse and wrathful disposition. All efforts should be made for the patient to have good sleep at night. Even rest during the day is essential. He should never be permitted to remain awake at night for long.

The patient's bowels should move regularly. If there is constipation, he is advised to take a glass of water early morning and go for a walk every day.

HIGH BLOOD PRESSURE

Blood is pumped by the heart to all parts of the body through the arteries, its branches and numerous capillaries. When the heart contracts, blood is forced into the arteries and thus, exerts a positive pressure on the walls of these channels. When the heart dilates, the pressure in the arteries is reduced and a negative pressure is created. The walls of the arteries are elastic to accommodate both positive and negative pressures. During contraction of the heart, the pressure exerted on the walls of the arteries is called systolic pressure, and during dilatation of the heart, the pressure exerted is called diastolic pressure.

Blood pressure varies from person to person depending upon age, sex, physical and mental work. Males, those who are aged and those who are exposed to more mental and physical work normally maintain higher blood pressure than others. In physiological conditions, blood pressure increases during fear, anger and excitement. A person during sleep and period of rest maintains a lower blood pressure.

Apart from the psychic and emotional factors mentioned above, blood pressure goes up because of the vitiation of *vayu.* Both the psychic and physical factors including climate are responsible for this morbidity. Excessive intake of salt, lack of exercise, mental worry, sleeplessness and diseases of the kidneys, among others, are responsible for high blood pressure, in old age; specially when the kidney is affected, blood pressure goes up. Because of accumulation of salts in the musculature of the walls of the arteries, their elasticity is reduced and thus, even a little force from the heart exerts pressure on them.

A person with high blood pressure does not sleep well at night. Palpitation, giddiness, a feeling of unstability, lack of equilibrium, dyspnoea on slight exertion, weakness and impairment of digestion are experienced. When high blood pressure becomes chronic, due to lack of elasticity of the vessels, the capillaries supplying blood to the eyes, specially to the retina are affected which results in local bleeding and impairment of vision. When the condition further aggravates, it affects the end-arteries supplying blood to the brain. Due to the lack of elasticity, they may rupture and bleeding takes place. This bleeding is commonly known as cerebral haemorrhage. This results in paralysis. Movement of the various organs of the body are regulated by their centres located in the brain. The centre affected by the haemorrhage is responsible for the paralysis of the corresponding organ in the body.

Treatment: All medicines which alleviate *vayu* and promote the strength of nervous system are useful in this condition. *Lasuna* or garlic is an excellent drug. Garlic produces a heating effect on the body when taken raw. Garlic made into a paste and mixed with buttermilk is very effective in the treatment of this condition. To begin with about one gm. of garlic should be administered three times a day. This should gradually be increased to 3 gm. three times a day. Another method which is popularly followed is to fry the garlic in ghee. This reduces the smell and makes it palatable.

Sarpagandha is commonly used in the treatment of high blood pressure by Ayurvedic physicians. The drug is also used very widely in the allopathic system of medicine. Many alkaloids have been isolated from this drug and they are found to be effective in reducing blood pressure. In Ayurveda, the root of this drug is used in its raw state. The powder of the drug is given to an adult patient in a dose of half teaspoonful three times a day. Tablets are prepared from the concentrated aqueous extract of this drug and may be given to the patient in a dose of two tablets three times a day. Isolated fractions (alkaloids), when taken alone for a long time, produce some adverse effects. Such adverse effects are not found when the whole drug is taken either in powder or tablet form.

For patients suffering from chronic hypertension, *dhara* therapy is considered to be the most effective. Medicated oil boiled with *bala* and milk is used in the therapy. This oil is kept in an earthen vessel hanging from a high pedestal or the roof of the house. The patient should lie on the ground on his back. The medicated oil is dripped on to the forehead of the patient (between the eye-brows), from a small hole made at the bottom of the earthen vessel. This is done once every day preferably in the morning for about half an hour. By the use of this therapy, the patient sleeps soundly at night and the blood pressure gradually comes down. The same oil is also used for massaging the head as well as the body. This oil, prepared by boiling *bala* with milk one hundred times, is known as *Shatavartita kshirabala taila.* Five drops of this oil should be given to the patient internally with a cup of milk every day. This is well-known for its effectiveness in reducing high blood pressure.

Diet: The patient should not be given hot and spicy food and should avoid salt as far as possible. Hydrogenated oils should be strictly avoided. The patient can be given ghee and butter prepared from cow's milk. The ghee and butter prepared of buffalo milk is not advisable. The patient should take such vegetables as could help him in keeping his bowels clear. Bitter gourd, drumsticks, *patola* and *bimbi* are the most useful vegetables.

Fig. 9 *Rauwolfia serpentina* (*sarpagandha*)

The patient should avoid colocasia and yellow variety of pumpkin. He can take all types of dry fruits. Orange, banana, guava and apples are considered very useful. Almond oil can be given in a dose of one teaspoonful at bedtime in a cup of warm milk. Almond oil can also be given for inhalation. This helps in soothing the nerves and thus, reduces blood pressure. Fruits and boiled vegetables are better than cereals and pulses for these patients.

Other regimens: The patient should not be permitted to remain awake for a long time at night, and he should be given as much rest as possible. Mental strain in any form should be avoided. He can undertake physical exercise to some extent, but heavy physical exercise specially lifting of heavy weights, etc., should be avoided. He should be regular in his habits of taking food and evacuating bowels. He should devote some time for prayer which gives mental peace and tranquillity.

JAUNDICE

Jaundice is characterised by the appearance of yellowness in the eyes and skin. In Ayurveda this is called *kamala.* It is caused by excessive circulation of *pitta* (bile pigments) in the blood. The liver is responsible for the production of *pitta.* If there is any obstruction in the bile duct, or impairment of the functions of the liver, or excessive destruction of the red blood cells, then the *pitta* appears in excess in the blood. Normally it comes out of the body through urine and stool. If, however, there is an obstruction in the bile ducts, then it does not come out through the bowels. Normal stool gets its characteristic colour because of the bile and if there is an obstruction in the bile duct then the stool becomes pale white in colour. The urine however, continues to be excessively yellow in all types of jaundice.

Apart from the yellowness of the eyes and the skin, many other symptoms are manifested depending upon the cause of the jaundice. The digestion, specially that of fat, is impaired, and consequently the patient becomes physically weak. Destruction of red blood cells, and circulation of bile pigments in excessive quantity result in the impairment of the oxidation of the tissue cells resulting in defective metabolism and associated complaints. There may be itching all over the body.

Treatment: In Ayurveda, in such conditions, purgation is administered in the beginning. Since the patient is weak, strong purgatives are contra-indicated. Only cholagogue type of purgatives which stimulate the function of the liver and increase the flow of bile in the bile duct are used. *Trivrit* and *kutaki* are the two drugs of choice for its treatment. The root bark of *trivrit* and the rhizome of *kutaki* are used separately or mixed together in a powder form. Depending upon the strength of the patient and the seriousness as well as the stage of the disease, the powder of these drugs is given in a dose of one to two teaspoonfuls, twice daily with hot water.

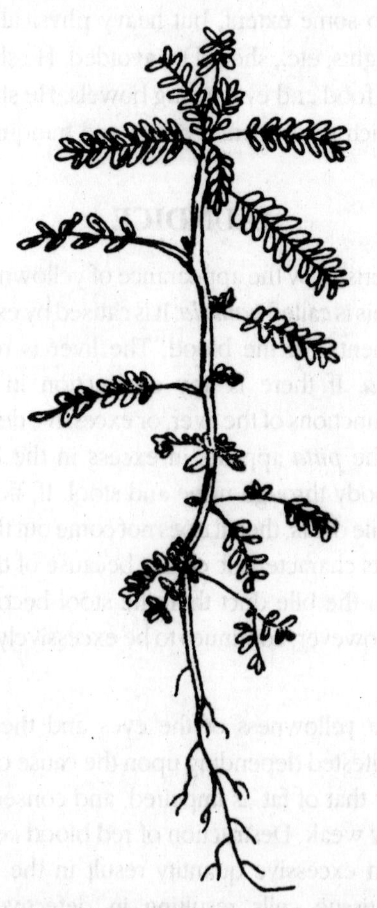

Fig. 10 *Phyllanthus niruri (bhumyamalaki)*

Two compound preparations frequently used in the treatment of this condition are *Avipattikara churna* and *Arogya vardhini vati. Trivrit* is an important ingredient of the former and *katuki* of the latter. The former which is in a powder form is given in a dose of one teaspoonful twice daily with hot water. The latter which is in the form of tablets (of 0.25 gm. each) is given in a dose of two tablets three times daily followed by hot water or mixed with honey.

Bhumyamalaki is commonly used in the treatment of all types of *kamala*. It is a small herb about six inches high. It has a slender and soft stalk. The juice of this plant is given to the patient in a dose of one teaspoonful three times a day, mixed with honey. This can also be given in the form of a paste. Other drugs which are also used in this condition are *vasaka, kakamachi* and *triphala*.

Diet: Sweet things and liquid foods like sugar-cane juice, orange juice and dry grapes are to be given to the patient in large quantities. This increases urination which helps in the elimination of bile pigments which are excessive in the blood. Vegetable and meat soups can be given to the patient. Vegetables having bitter taste are useful in this condition. Food articles which are sour and pungent in taste and spices are not good for this condition. Salt should be taken in limited quantity. Pomegranate, although sour, is good. Curd should not be given. But butter-milk prepared by churning the curd and removing the butter can be given to the patient in large quantities provided it is not very sour. Alcohol in any form is contra-indicated.

Other regimens: The patient should be given complete rest. He should avoid heat, sun, sex and psychic factors like anger and anxiety.

OEDEMA

In the body, oedema or non-inflammatory swelling takes place due to several reasons. Ailments of the heart, liver and kidney as well as anaemia are some of the important causes of oedema. In all types of oedema, whatever its cause may be there is accumulation of water inside the tissues in excess. This is required to be taken out of the body.

Treatment: *Punarnava* is the drug of choice for the treatment of this condition. It is a short creeper and is available almost everywhere in India except in high altitudes. It grows luxuriously after the onset of rains. In some places, people use this plant as a leafy vegetable. It is of two types, the red and the white. Both of them are used in medicine. The whole plant is given to the patient, but its roots act better than other parts of this plant in curing oedema. Very popularly used preparation in cases of oedema is known as *Punarnava mandura.* It is an iron preparation to which *punarnava* is added. It is normally available in a powder form and given to the patient in varying doses depending upon the cause of the disease and its acuteness. Normally 2 gm. of this drug is given to the patient, three times a day, mixed with honey. It gives a black colour to the stool. If there is constipation, it indirectly helps to relieve it and certain amount of fluid goes out of the body through stools. It improves the function of the kidneys and promotes urination.

An alcoholic preparation of this drug is known as *Punarnavadyarishta.* Six teaspoonfuls of this liquid are given to the patient after food, twice daily. It should be diluted by adding equal quantity of water before it is administered to the patients. If the oedema is caused because of liver ailment, then this liquid should be used in smaller quantity.

Along with this medicine, other medicines which are required to cure the cause of the oedema should also be administered simultaneously.

Diet: Salt, fried things and curd are strictly prohibited. Vegetables like drumstick, green banana, gourd, *patola,* bitter gourd are useful for such types of patients. If there is constipation, the patient should be given ripe papaya in good quantity. Green papaya is also useful as a vegetable for this condition. Excess of fat either of vegetable origin or of animal origin should be avoided. Groundnut oil and its preparations are strictly prohibited.

Other regimens: The patient is well advised not to sleep during daytime. In all types of oedema, if he feels fatigued, he can take rest, but his eyes should remain open. As far as possible, he should move about and avoid sedentary habits.

SCURVY

This is caused by the deficiency of Vitamin C and is marked, by weakness, anaemia, spongy gums and mucocutaneous haemorrhages. Bleeding occurs primarily from the gums. It may also occur from the capillaries inside the skin. The presence of Vitamin C is very essential for coagulation

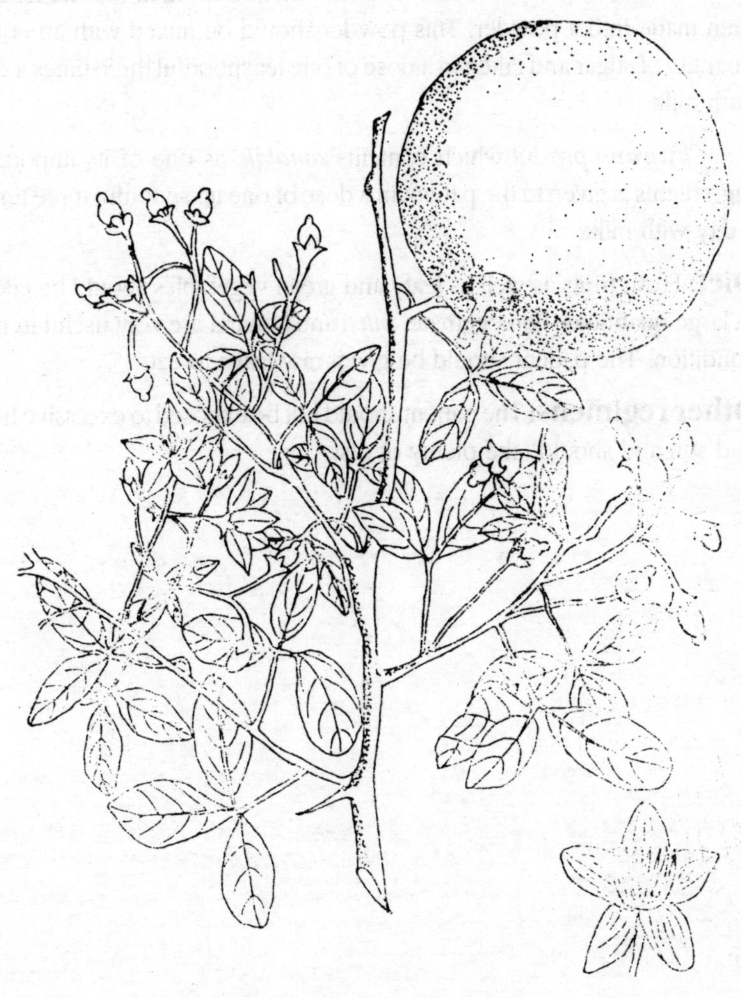

Fig. 11 *Aegle marmelos* (*bilva*)

of blood. In its absence, blood does not coagulate and the capillary walls become fragile. They rupture very easily and bleeding does not stop even after a prolonged period. This usually occurs among people in the army and also among people who live on tinned or preserved foods. Excessive boiling of vegetables destroys Vitamin C and people accustomed to this type of food are prone to suffer from this ailment.

Treatment *Amalaki* is the drug of choice for the treatment of this condition. The ripe fruit should be collected and dried in the shade. It is then made into a powder. This powder should be mixed with an equal quantity of sugar and taken in a dose of one teaspoonful three times a day with milk.

Chyavana prasha which contains *amalaki* as one of its important ingredients is given to the patient in a dose of one teaspoonful three times a day with milk.

Diet: Fresh fruits as well as leafy and green vegetables should be taken in large quantities. Pomegranate, *bilva* and banana are very useful in this condition. The patient should be given raw fruits to eat.

Other regimens: The patient should not be exposed to excessive heat and sun and should take plenty of rest.

CHAPTER 8

DISEASES OF EYE

CATARACT

Opacification of the lens or its capsule sufficient to interfere with the vision of the eye is called cataract. In Ayurveda this disease is called *timira* or *linga nasha.* Aggravated *vayu* is considered to be responsible for the manifestation of this disease. One of the properties of *vayu* is to make things dry up. When the unctuousness and softness of the lens and its capsule are lost, it becomes opaque and the rays of light coming from the object are unable to pass through this. When the rays do not pass through this, the retina becomes incapable of accepting them. Thereby, the perception of vision is impaired. In the first stage of the cataract the whole lens or the capsule may not be affected and thus, there will be only partial impairment of vision. The object may appear disrupted or dull.

Treatment: The aggravated *vayu* has to be corrected first. Ghee is one of the important articles which corrects *vayu*. *Triphala* provides nourishment and strengthens the nerves and other tissues of the eye ball. *Maha Triphala ghrita* consisting of ghee with *triphala*, among others, is popularly used for the treatment of this condition. If the cataract is fully matured, then it is very difficult to correct it. This medicine, therefore, acts very well only in the first stage of the development of this condition. This medicated ghee is given to the patient in a dose of two teaspoonfuls, twice daily, about one hour before taking food mixed with a cup of warm milk.

Chandrodaya varti is used externally in this condition. Over a clean stone it is rubbed with a little water and the paste is applied in the form of a collyrium. It is a slight irritant. Therefore it promotes blood circulation and lacrimation in the eyes. The collyrium also provides nourishment to the tissues of the eye.

For prevention of this disease and also for curing when it has just started, *triphala* water is very useful. *Triphala* powder should be taken in a dose of one tablespoonful and added to a tumblerful of water in the evening. This is kept for 12 hours, well covered. In the morning, this should be squeezed and strained through a piece of clean cloth. The filtrate, thus obtained, should be used both for washing the eyes and taking internally.

To keep the eyes free from any disease it is necessary to keep the patient free from constipation. Both *Maha Triphala ghrita* and *triphala* water help in keeping the patient free from constipation.

Diet: Cow's ghee, milk and butter are useful. The patient can take rice, wheat, *moong* dal, banana (both ripe and green), *methi,* spinach, *patola,* sweet variety of *koshataki,* drumsticks, lady's fingers, grapes, pomegranates, apples and oranges. Pungent, bitter, sour and saline ingredients of food should be avoided. Sea-salt should never be used even in vegetables. Only rock-salt should be used, that too in a small quantity.

Other regimens: Exposure to excessive heat and sun is prohibited. Excessive worry, anxiety and anger help in the aggravation of *vayu* and *pitta* which help in causing the disease. They should therefore be avoided.

MYOPIA

Myopia generally occurs in the young and patient experiences difficulty in seeing objects at a distance. This is because of the parallel rays transmitted by the objects, focusing in front of the retina. This may be due to the change in the curvature of the refracting surface of the eye or due to abnormal refractivity of the media of the eye.

Normally after the use of spectacles with concave lens of appropriate curvature, the patient is relieved of the trouble. But he should continue to use the spectacles. In one type of myopia, the morbidity continues to increase in adult life. This is called "progressive myopia" and the patient goes on changing his lens for higher numbers. In Ayurveda this condition is known as '*drishti dosha*'.

In Ayurveda, persons suffering from chronic cold and constipation are considered to be more prone to get myopia. Nervous debility is also considered to give rise to this trouble.

It begins by the patient getting a blurred vision of the matter written on a black-board or shown on a screen. The patient experiences a little difficulty in recognising persons a short distance away. He also experiences difficulties when reading continuously for some time. There may be watering from the eyes, itching and a feeling of heaviness and burning sensation in the eye-balls. This may also result in headache and disturbance in sleep.

Treatment: While treating this condition, care is always taken to cure the patient of his chronic cold and constipation, if present. *Triphala* is commonly used by Ayurvedic physicians for the treatment of this condition. One tablespoonful of this powder is added to a tumblerful of water in the evening and kept overnight. In the early morning the powder should be strained through a clean cloth and thrown away. The water, thus obtained, should be used both for sprinkling over the eyes and drinking. About 120 ml. of this water should be taken internally. In the case of some individuals, it may cause loose motions, and in some other persons it may not have any effect at all on the bowels. Therefore, the dose of this water should be so regulated that the person gets one clear motion in the early morning. It may take two to three days to regulate the dose. After this is taken for about 15 days, and after the constipative tendency is removed, it no longer produces loose motions. This dosage has to be continued for about 3 months for tonic effect on the eye. This water should be sprinkled gently over the eyeballs in the early morning.

Yashti madhu is the other medicine of choice for the treatment of this condition. The root or rhizome of this plant is used for the purpose of medicine. It is very fibrous. Therefore, preparing a powder of this requires a lot of work. One teaspoonful of this should be mixed with 1/2 a teaspoon of pure ghee and one teaspoonful of pure honey. This should be taken twice daily on an empty stomach — once in the morning before breakfast, and once in the afternoon before tea when the stomach is nearly empty. If myopia is caused because of nervous debility then a compound preparation of this drug called *Saptamrita lauha* is used. In this compound preparation *triphala, yashti madhu, lauha bhasma*, ghee and honey are used. One teaspoonful of this powder is added to a cup of milk and taken twice a day.

To check progressive myopia, the medicated ghee prepared by boiling *triphala* and some other drugs is used. This is called *Maha Triphala ghrita*. If cow's ghee is used for preparing this medicine it produces exceedingly good results in a short time. One teaspoonful of this ghee is to be used twice daily with milk. If there is constipative tendency, then the dose of this ghee should be increased up to 3 teaspoonfuls, two times daily.

To cure the patient of cold and nasal congestion, a medicated oil, prepared by boiling some medicines with mustard oil, called *Shadbindu taila* is used. Six drops of this oil are dropped into each nostril of the nose and deeply inhaled once in the morning. In the beginning, this inhalation may cause a little irritation in the nose and sneezing. But when habitually used, this does not occur.

Diet: Pungent and sour articles of food like spices, pickles and curd are contra-indicated. Foods which cause constipation and nasal congestion should be avoided. Cow's ghee is considered to be very useful in this condition. It can be taken along with the food. Fried things are not useful in this condition.

Other regimens: The patient should not strain his eyes during his studies. He should give a little rest to the eyes after reading a few pages. Writing during the night should be avoided as far as possible. Needlework and painting are also considered to put lot of strain on the eye. While reading, proper posture should be maintained and the book should be kept at a distance by which it can be read comfortably. Reading while lying on the bed is contra-indicated. The patient is prohibited from keeping awake at night especially for the purpose of studying and witnessing film shows. A walk in the early morning for about 3 kilometres daily is very helpful in arresting the progress of this trouble.

STYE

This is a small inflamed tumour on the eye-lid. It is usually caused because of poor health, conjunctivitis, infection in the eye-lids, and lack of cleanliness. They cause pain and uneasiness. It takes about 5-8 days for this little tumour in the eye-lid to suppurate and once the pus comes out of it, the patient feels relieved and the whole thing subsides. There is a tendency for the styes to appear again and again.

Treatment: According to Ayurveda, constipation is attributed to be one of the common causes of stye. Therefore, before starting the treatment, the patient is given the purgative. Usually *triphala* powder is chosen for this purpose. The patient should be given one teaspoonful of this *triphala* powder at bedtime with a cup of hot milk. Another spoon of the powder should be added to a tumblerful of water and kept overnight. Next morning, it should be squeezed and filtered, and the liquid thus obtained, is to be used for washing the eyes. To prevent relapse of this disease a collyrium is frequently prescribed by the Ayurvedic physicians. This is known as *Chandrodaya varti*. It is available in rod-shaped round pieces with the ends tapering. This is to be rubbed with a few drops of honey over a clean stone or plate and the collyrium thus prepared, is to be applied over the eyes gently. It causes a little irritation and thus there is watering from the eyes. But this irritation stops in about 5-10 minutes after its application.

Diet: The patient should avoid all sour foods and drinks. Curd are specially prohibited. Bitter things and things which are useful for getting a clean motion are always prescribed for such patients.

Other regimens: The patient should not remain awake for long at night. Reading is not advisable. He should also avoid the sun. He should not take head bath or expose himself to extreme cold winds and rain.

CHAPTER 9

DISEASES OF GENITAL ORGANS

FEMALE STERILITY

THE UNION of sperm and ovum and their implantation in the wall of the uterus leads to the development of the foetus. For the proper development of a foetus, proper nourishment should be provided through the mother, and the mother should be free from disease during the period of conception and gestation. Sterility in females is, therefore, a result of either the impairment of the ovary, uterus, fallopian tubes or hormones controlling the functions of these organs as well as disease of the would-be mother.

Defects in the genital organs may be structural (organic) or functional. To correct organic defects surgical measures have to be taken. Functional defects of these organs can be successfully treated by Ayurvedic medicines. The condition is called *bandhyatva* in Ayurveda, and generally, this is caused by the simultaneous aggravation of all the three *doshas.*

Treatment: *Phala ghrita* is very effective in the treatment of this condition. It is given to the patient in a dose of two teaspoonfuls twice daily on an empty stomach, mixed with milk. *Vanga bhasma* is the medicine of choice for the treatment of this condition. It is given to the patient in a dose of 0.125 gm. twice daily, mixed with honey. *Shilajit* is one of the most effective drugs for the cure of sterility. It is given to the patient in a dose of one teaspoonful twice daily.

Bala is used both locally and internally. The root of this plant is boiled in oil and milk. It is used with lukewarm water as a douche. This brings about a change in the mucous membrane of the genital tract which aids the effective combination of ovum and sperm in the uterus. This medicated oil is also used internally in a dose of one teaspoonful in the morning with a cup of milk.

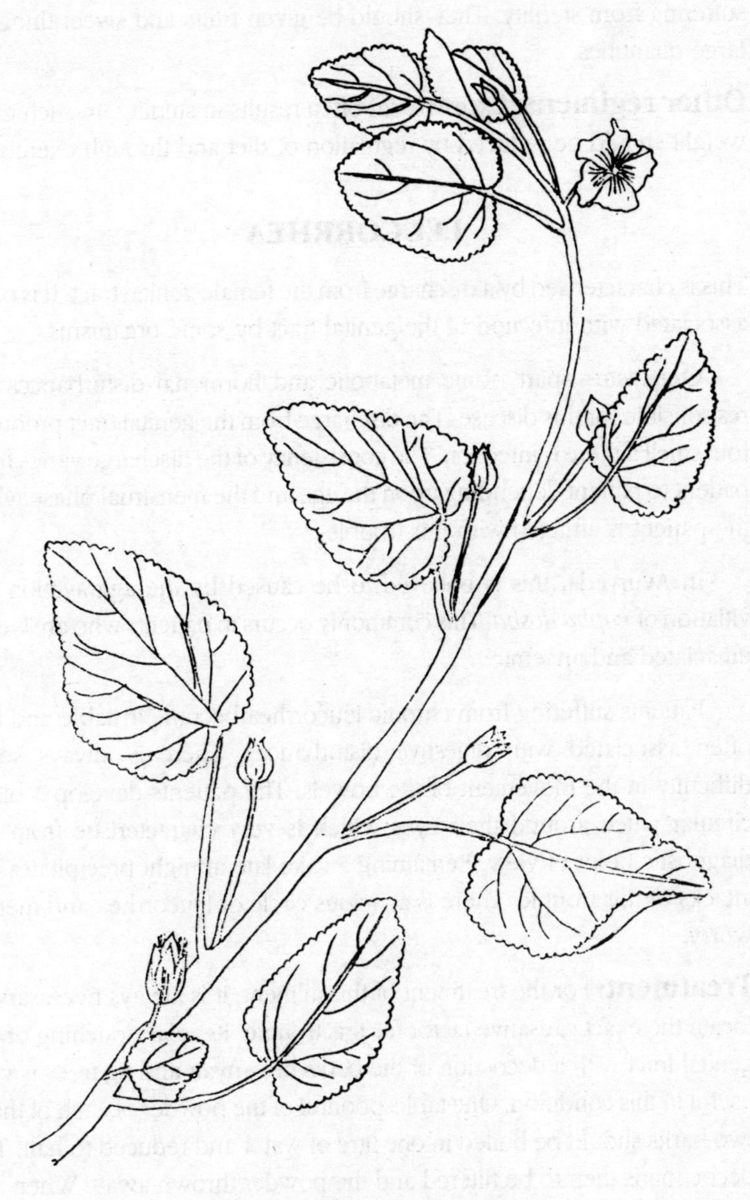

Fig. 12 *Sida rhombifolia* (*bala*)

Diet: Alkaline and pungent food should not be taken by persons suffering from sterility. They should be given fruits and sweet things in large quantities.

Other regimens: Excessive fat often results in sterility. In such cases weight should be reduced by regulation of diet and through exercise.

LEUCORRHEA

This is characterised by a discharge from the female genital tract. It is often associated with infection of the genital tract by some organisms.

Organisms apart, some metabolic and hormonal disturbances are responsible for this disease. The discharge from the genital tract produces foul smell if there is infection. The consistency of the discharge varies from patient to patient depending upon the age and the menstrual phase when the patient is afflicted with this trouble.

In Ayurveda, this is believed to be caused by the aggravation or vitiation of *kapha dosha*. This commonly occurs in patients who are weak, emaciated and anaemic.

Patients suffering from chronic leucorrhea become irritable and it is often associated with digestive disturbances. There is always some difficulty in the movement of the bowels. The patients develop a black circular patch around their eyes which is very characteristic from the diagnostic point of view. Remaining awake late at night precipitates the attacks of this trouble. There is a vicious circle of leucorrhea and mental worry.

Treatment: For the treatment of this ailment, it is always necessary to locate the exact causative factor for this trouble. Regular douching of the genital tract with a decoction of the barks of banyan and fig trees is very useful in this condition. One tablespoonful of the powder of each of these two barks should be boiled in one litre of water and reduced to half. The decoction is then to be filtered and the powder thrown away. When it is slightly warm, douching should be performed. This decoction keeps the tissue cells of this area healthy. The popular medicine used by Ayurvedic physicians in this condition is *Pradarantaka lauha.* This drug contains some *bhasmas* of metals. The most important one is the *bhasma* of iron. For the preparation of this medicine, the ingredients are triturated with the juice of *kumari.* 250 mg. of this drug is given to the patient three times a day, with honey.

Kumari is also used in the treatment of this condition. It tones up the tissue cells of the uterus and the genital tract and prevents exudation of abnormal fluid. *Kumari* is planted in the hedge of gardens. When fully matured this plant produces beautiful pink flowers. It grows luxuriantly in sandy areas. When the outer skin of the leaf of this plant is removed, a fleshy pulp comes out which is used for the extraction of juice. 30 ml. of this is to be given to the patient twice daily with a little honey added to it, preferably on an empty stomach. This juice stimulates the liver, promotes digestion and regulates the bowels. It has some effect in correcting the hormonal imbalances by which genital organs of the patient get toned up.

Lodhra is also used for the purpose of douching. The bark of this tree is used and the decoction of the bark is prepared on the lines suggested above. This medicine is also used in the form of *lodhra asava.* The alcoholic soluble fraction of this drug is extracted through a special process during which some other drugs are added to it. 30 ml. of this drug is given to the patient twice daily after food, with equal quantity of water. *Sphatika* or alum is also used both externally and internally for the treatment of this condition. Alum is fried in a vessel over fire and then powdered. One teaspoonful of this powder is added to the decoctions described above and used for the purpose of douching. 125 mg. of this powder is mixed with 125 mg. of *pradarantaka lauha* and given to the patient twice daily on an empty stomach mixed with honey. Along with all the medicines described above *tandulodaka* (rice-wash) is given as a means to accelerate their action. Rice-wash alone is useful for the cure of this disease.

Diet: Fried and spicy food should not be given to the patient. The patient should not be permitted to keep her stomach empty for a long time. She should not take heavy, indigestible food articles. Sour things especially pickles and curd are prohibited. Intake of *supari* (areca nut) after taking food is very useful both for prevention and cure of this disease.

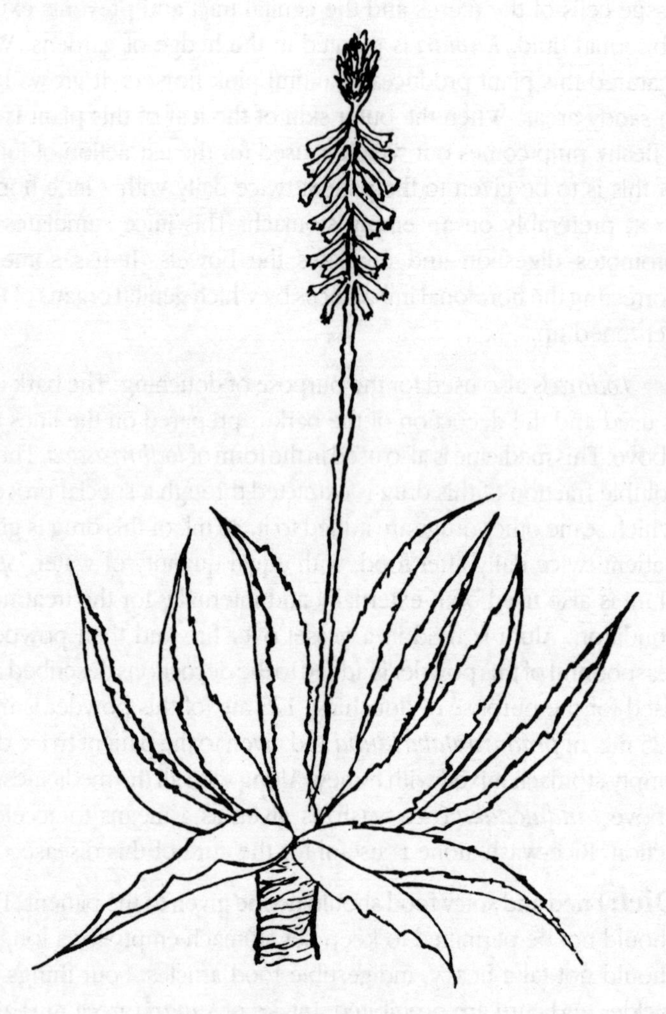

Fig. 13 *Aloe barbadensis* (*kumari*)

Other regimens: The patient should be free from worries and should not keep herself awake late in the night. Sexual intercourse during the attack of this disease is prohibited. A brisk walk in the early morning helps in the early cure of this disease. Sanitary and hygienic measures should be followed carefully.

MALE STERILITY

The condition in which a married couple finds it difficult to produce an offspring is called sterility. The defect may be either with the male partner or the female partner. These defects can be either organic or functional. In males the procreative factor is the sperm. It is produced in the testicles and ejaculated through the male genital organ during sexual intercourse. The production of sperm is regulated by hormones which are secreted by the ductless glands of the body. For the procreation of offspring, the sperm should be active and they should be in sufficient numbers in the semen. Sometimes because of some morbidity, sperm is either absent in the semen or small in number. In such cases conception does not take place.

Treatment: The condition in which the sperm does not exist in the semen is difficult to treat. But if the sperms are present, but they are either few in number, or inactive, the condition can be easily remedied.

Ashvagandha is the ideal drug for the treatment of this condition. The root of this plant is used. It is cultivated in some parts of the country but is available in all parts of the country as jungle weed. Its root, when fresh, has a smell like that of the urine of the horse. Hence its name is *ashvagandha*. The dried root of this plant does not have any smell, and can be taken without much inconvenience. It can either be taken as powder in a dose of one teaspoonful twice daily followed by a cup of milk each time, or it can be boiled with milk and then taken. To make it palatable it can be mixed with sugar syrup. This preparation is called *Ashvagandha lehya*. It becomes a linctus and can be given to the patient in a dose of one teaspoonful twice daily followed by a cup of milk. One alcoholic preparation of this medicine is called *Ashvagandharishta*. It is given to the patient in a dose of 30 ml. twice daily after food with equal quantity of water.

Fig. 14 *Withania somnifera* (*ashvagandha*)

The other drug useful in this condition is *kapikacchu.* It is a creeper which grows all over the country. The seeds which are inside the pods of this plant are used in the medicine. They are roasted and made into powder. One teaspoonful of the powder of this drug is given to the patient twice daily followed by a cup of milk each time.

Makaradhvaja is the most important medicine which is commonly used by Ayurvedic physicians in the treatment of this and allied conditions. It is prepared by a special process through the combination of mercury, sulphur and gold. 125 mg. of this medicine are given to the patient twice daily on an empty stomach mixed with half a teaspoonful of butter and half a teaspoonful of sugar.

All these above mentioned medicines, apart from their spermatopoetic and spermatogenetic properties, are very good tonics for the nerves and the heart. They do not produce any adverse effect even if used for a long time. They, however, produce warmth in the body. Thus, they are ideal for the winter season.

Diet: Saline, sour, pungent and bitter things are not good for this condition. Food ingredients having sweet and astringent tastes are normally administered to the patients. Sweet things like milk, ghee and butter are useful. Meat or eggs can be given to the patient in good quantity. Cow's milk and ghee prepared from it is considered to be specially useful in the treatment of this condition.

Other regimens: All medicines which produce active sperms of better quality are usually aphrodisiacs, i.e., they are sex stimulants. The individual should, however, take care not to indulge in sex too frequently. Restraint in sex is always good for this condition.

MENORRHAGIA

Excessive bleeding during menstruation is called menorrhagia. In Ayurveda, this is known as *rakta pradara.*

Due to an impairment of the hormones excessive bleeding takes place during menstruation. This impairment is caused by the aggravation of *pitta.* There are other conditions such as cancer of the uterus and many other blood diseases in which menorrhagia occurs.

Menstruation may start with pain in abdomen, the lumber region, or hips. If excessive bleeding continues for long period, the patient will feel exceedingly weak and debilitated. Giddiness, headache, pain in the calf and restlessness may occur. The patient becomes anaemic and may experience palpitation of the heart. This may also be associated with breathlessness.

Treatment: *Ashoka* and *lodhra* are popularly used for the treatment of this condition. The powder of the barks of these two are given to the patient either separately or in a compound form in a dose of one teaspoonful four times a day, with cold water. *Ashokarishta* and *Lodhrasava* are two important preparations of these drugs. They are given to the patient in a dose of 30 ml. twice daily after food with an equal quantity of water.

The tender leaves of the pomegranate tree are used for the treatment of this condition. Seven leaves along with seven grains of rice are made into a paste and given to the patient twice daily for a month. This works both as a preventive as well as a curative medicine.

Pravala and *mukta* are used in acute attacks of this disease. They are given in a powder form which is called *pishti.* 100 mg. of the powder of this drug is given to the patient four times a day.

Diet: Old rice, wheat, *moong dal,* milk and ghee can be given to the patient. Sugarcane juice, grapes, jack-fruit, banana, *amalaki* and pomegranate are very useful in this condition. Hot and spicy things are to be strictly avoided.

Other regimens: The patient should not resort to any exercise, hard or light. She should take complete rest. Worry, anxiety and anger aggravate this condition and therefore complete mental and physical rest should be taken. Exposure to the sun, heat, riding vehicles, and long journeys should be avoided. While sleeping, the foot of the bed of the patient should be raised a little.

PAINFUL MENSTRUATION

In Ayurveda, this is known as *rajah-kricchra.* Ayurveda attributes painful menstruation to the predominance of *doshas*, namely, *vayu, pitta* and *kapha.* The pain may appear before the menstruation starts and may subside thereafter. It may also continue till the end of menstruation. The pain affects different organs of the lower pelvic region and at times, it becomes severe. There might be nausea, vomiting, loss of appetite and constipation. The sleep of the patient may also get disturbed.

Treatment: In Ayurveda lower pelvis is considered to be the seat of *apana vayu*, which is responsible for the elimination of menstrual blood, stool, urine, ovum and sperm (in males). Women having constipating tendency or those who do not develop regular habit of attending the call of nature, are usually exposed to this type of complaint. The Ayurvedic physician, therefore, suggests a purgative to be given to the patient for about two days before the scheduled date of menstruation. *Kumari* is the drug of choice for the treatment of this condition. From its pulp the juice is extracted and given to the patient. Sometimes the juice is dehydrated and given to the patient. Sometimes the juice is dehydrated and the stuff that is obtained by this, is used in the medicine. This plant grows in all parts of India, but it has a luxurious growth in deserts and rocky places.

Kumari asava, which is an alcoholic preparation of this drug, is given to the patient in a dose of 6 teaspoonfuls, twice daily after food with equal quantity of water. *Rajah pravartani* which contains borax in *bhasma* form, asafoetida and *kumari*, is also an effective drug. Two tablets of this medicine are given to the patient, twice a day for about 7 days, immediately before the due date of menses. It relieves congestion in the pelvic organs, works as a laxative and thus keeps the patient free from any pain during menstruation.

Pain during menstruation might be caused due to some organic defect in the female genital tract. In that case, surgery is the only way out. Medicines prescribed above will be helpful only if the pain is caused by functional defects.

Diet: The patient should not be given fried things, pulses and sour things.

Last week of the menstrual cycle is very crucial for these patients. They should not take anything that will cause constipation. Vegetables like colocasia, potato, yellow pumpkin and brinjal are to be avoided. White pumpkin, papaya, *surana*, drumstick, gourd, bitter gourd and cucumber are useful. Garlic is specially recommended. Women having this type of complaint should use garlic in a dose of 10 cloves, twice a day. The outer coating of garlic should be removed and it should be cut into pieces. The pungent smell of garlic is reduced if a little bit of butter-milk or lime juice is added to it. If, however, the patient is unable to tolerate the residual smell of garlic, it should be fried with a little butter and given.

As has been told before, impairment of *apana vayu* is primarily responsible for this trouble. Its normal course is downwards and if it does not move because of hormonal imbalance, constipation, or any other factors, the best thing to do is to add sufficient quantity of asafoetida to the food of the patient. It can be given to the patient in a powder form and for this it has to be fried with ghee or butter in a big spoon over fire. This makes it brittle and powder can be made out of it conveniently. This powder should be taken in a dose of 1 teaspoonful, twice daily along with food. It should be followed by hot water. Because of the pungent smell it emits, some people do not like to take it alone. It may be added with butter-milk or vegetables or rice or bread and taken by the patient.

Other regimens: Women having sedentary habits are more prone to this trouble. They should, therefore, be treated psychologically. The patient should be asked to be in the company of friends and relatives, specially during the period. She should find an opportunity for walking at least 3-4 kilometres a day. Morning walk is extremely useful for this condition. If she is fat, effort should be made to reduce weight. Some physical exercises involving the bending of the waist region and contraction of the pelvic muscles should be resorted to regularly. Sleep during daytime is extremely harmful. During the period of menstruation, she should take complete rest.

CHAPTER 10

PSYCHIC DISEASES AND DISEASES OF NERVOUS SYSTEM

CRAMPS

An involuntary and painful contraction of a voluntary muscle or a groups of muscles, is known as cramp. In Ayurveda this is known as *mamsagata vayu*. When it is confined to calf muscles of the leg, it is called *pindiko-dveshtana*. Carrying out exercises much in excess of one's own capacity, indulgence in dry and rough food articles and taking some harmful medicines may result in its attack. Of the types of *vayu, vyana vayu* pervades all over the body and among other functions it regulates the functions of voluntary muscles. This regulates the functions of the cerebro-spinal nervous system. If any metabolic waste which normally should be eliminated from the body does not get out, and circulates inside the body, it is likely to get deposited between nerve-endings and the muscle tissue. This in Ayurvedic parlance is known an *ama,* which is responsible for the causation of these cramps. Cramps are also caused as symptoms of different other diseases.

Treatment: Massage is the best therapy for correcting *vyana vayu*. It should be done by rubbing medicated oil like *Mahanarayana taila* all over the body. In winter season, it should be made warm by heating and then applied for massage. Those who get cramps frequently can even use ordinary gingelly oil and have a massage by themselves, before taking daily bath.'

Simhanada guggulu is a good drug for the treatment of this condition. These patients are usually constipated. *Simhanada guggulu* relieves constipation when given in a higher dose.

Normally it is given in a dose of 4 tablets, three times a day; but it can be increased further. Some hot drink, preferably hot milk should be given to the patient after he has taken this medicine.

If constipation is not relieved adequately by this medicine, the patient should be given castor oil in appropriate dose depending upon the constitution of the individual.

Diet: The patient should not be given such foods that aggravate *vayu*. Pulses are bad for such patients. Cold, rough, dry, pungent and astringent food item are bad for such patients. Sweet and sour things can be given to the patient in good quantity. Garlic, asafoetida and *patola* as vegetables are very useful.

Other regimens: The patient should resort to regular massage and exercise. He should not expose himself to cold wind or rain. Fasting, exercises in excess of one's own strength, remaining awake at night, suppression of natural urges, worry, anxiety and anger are some of the important causes of aggravation of *vayu*, and they should be discouraged. He should not sleep during daytime.

EPILEPSY

According to Ayurveda, diseases can be grouped into three categories depending upon the affliction of the mind and the body. They are: (1) Physical or somatic; (2) Psychosomatic; and (3) Psychic.

Anaemia or *pandu roga* belongs to the first category, bronchial asthma or *tamaka shwasa* belongs to the second category and epilepsy or *apasmara* belongs to the third category.

Depending upon the dominance of *doshas*, viz., *vata, pitta, kapha* and their combined form, *apasmara* is of four types. The fifth type is called *yoshapasmara*, which is popularly known as hysteria. This type is more prevalent among women. Various types of psychic stress are considered to be the causes of this disease and the heart interlinked with mind is primarily affected. Some physical factors like constipation, wind in stomach and impairment of digestion are precipitating factors.

Treatment: The aim of Ayurvedic treatment of this condition is to correct the nervous system and strengthen the heart. *Brahmi* and *vacha* are the two choice medicinal plants which Ayurvedic physicians use for treatment of this condition. Both these plants grow in marshy lands, specially near the sides of rivulets and streams. The entire plant of *brahmi* is used in medicine whereas only the rhizome or the underground portion of *vacha* is used. Stems and leaves of *brahmi* are thick and juicy, and they do not get dry easily. Therefore, the juice of this plant is used in medicine. On the other hand, the rhizome of *vacha* is used in powder form for which it should be dried in shade.

Fig. 15 *Bacopu monnieri (brahmi)*

One teaspoonful of the juice of *brahmi* or the powder of *vacha* or both combined is to be mixed with one teaspoonful of honey and given to the patient three times a day. Juice of *brahmi* is slightly bitter in taste and the addition of honey makes it palatable. The powder of *vacha* has an acrid smell and the addition of honey removes this bad smell and makes it more palatable.

There are many preparations of these two and other drugs. Some of them produce results quickly and there is no unpleasant taste and smell. One of the compound preparations which produces quicker results is *Brihat-vata-kulantaka rasa.* This drug, among others, contains gold in *bhasma* form. Various types of pharmaceutical processes through which this and such other metals are treated, make them non-toxic and easily assimilable. In 125 gm. dose, this medicine is to be given three times a day with honey.

Diet: Intake of pungent things is strictly prohibited. Cow's ghee is considered to be extremely beneficial in this condition. Deep inhalation of cow's ghee through nostrils also yields very good results.

Other regimens: Mental strain of all types should be avoided and the patient should always be kept busy so that he does not get time to brood over his ailment. Massage of the head and soles of the feet daily with *til* oil also contributes to a quick recovery from this trouble.

FACIAL PARALYSIS

Like any part of the body, the muscles of the face are supplied with nerves which control their action. These nerves at their outlet from the skull get compressed because of some local inflammation. Thus, there is impairment in the action of these nerves. This inflammation is often caused by exposure to cold wind and unwholesome diet.

The first sign of the facial paralysis is that the patient feels the face to be stiff and experiences difficulty is moving it. When paralysis sets in, the paralysed side becomes numb and motionless. The patient cannot close his eyes, and tears come out of them. He experiences difficulty in drinking and eating food.

The paralysis may be complete or incomplete. In the latter type usually the lower side of the face is affected.

Treatment : Hot fomentation with the help of a bolus by keeping salt in it is extremely useful in this condition. This should be kept over a frying pan, and heated. It should be tolerably hot and should be tested with fingers before it is applied to the patient. The facial nerve comes out of the skull through a hole below the lobule of the ear. It is, therefore, necessary to give fomentation on this part of the face. The fomentation should be for about half an hour twice a day. The face should never be exposed to cold wind. The spot should always be kept covered with a woollen muffler or a scarf. Massage of *Mahanarayana taila* is useful in this condition. The entire half of the face which is affected has to be given massage. The oil should be made tolerably warm before the massage, and the patient should be advised to keep himself indoors for about one hour. The massage should be gentle and slow.

Internally, the patient should be given *Vatagajankusha*. This is available in pill form and two pills of this medicine should be given to the patient three times a day, with honey. The pill should be made to a powder and thoroughly mixed with honey and given to the patient. *Dashamularishta* has a peculiar effect on nervous system. It tones up the nerves and helps them to work better. It has anti-inflammatory properties also. It is given in a dose of six teaspoonfuls twice a day, after food. with equal quantity of water. These medicines should be continued either separately, or together for about two weeks after the recovery of the paralysis. Since the condition is not very painful, the patient stops the treatment after he gets some relief and the residual paralysis which is left untreated, continues to be with him for the rest of his life. It is, therefore, necessary to take complete treatment and continue the treatment for about two weeks even after complete recovery. This is necessary with a view to preventing relapse of this condition.

The medicines mentioned above will work well only if the patient is not constipated. If he is constipated, castor oil should be given to him regularly as a purgative. Apart from purgation castor oil has got some anti-inflammatory property of the fibers, bones and joints. Thus it helps the patient very much.

Diet: Thc patient should avoid curd, sour and cold things, including ice-cream, chilled cola, iced beer and alcoholic drinks. Pulses of any type and their preparations will not be good for the patient. Among the vegetable, yellow pumpkin and colocasia are harmful for the patient. Leafy vegetable are very good in this condition. The patient should take wheat rather than rice. Cow's milk, are very useful for the patient.

Other regimens: The patient should not expose himself to rain or cold wind. He should also keep the face properly covered in winter season. Since he will not be able to close his eyes, even during his sleep they remain open, their is every possibility of foreign bodies, including germs, getting into them. Proper care should be taken to protect the eyes from this ailment. Remaining awake at night for a long time is very harmful to the patient.

LOSS OF MEMORY

Memory consists of remembering what has previously been learned. For example, when some one remembers a person's name, for example, he demonstrates both that he learned the name at some previous time and he had retained it during the intervening time when he might never have once thought of it. Retention is inactive, remembering is active and both are included under the general head of memory.

Ayurveda considers both body and mind to be closely inter linked. According to Ayurveda, no phenomenon is exclusively physical or mental. The body or mind might predominate in one case and might work as a secondary factor in another case. Thus, for good memory as also for the treatment of loss of memory, both psychic and physical factors are held to be effective.

Treatment: When the power of learning and remembering is impaired, to correct it, a drug called *brahmi* is popularly used. It is of two types — one variety is called *matsyakshi* and the other variety is called *mandukaparni.* Both these herbs are equally useful in improving memory.

They grow in marshy land near perennial streams. The juice of these plants is used in medicine. About 30 ml. of the juice is given to the patient twice daily on an empty stomach. Both of these are bitter and astringent. It is therefore administered with some honey to make it palatable. The fat soluble fraction of this drug is useful as a promoter of memory. Cow's ghee is well-known for its tonic effect on both the heart and the brain. Therefore, medicated ghee is prepared by boiling *brahmi*, along with some other drugs, in pure cow's ghee. This preparation is called *Brahmighrita*. One teaspoonful of this ghee is given to the patient twice daily on an empty stomach. This medicated ghee is added to a cup of warm milk, mixed with sugar, and taken after stirring well till it melts and gets well mixed with the milk. This preparation is found to be more useful when the patient suffering from loss of memory is emaciated.

The other drug used by Ayurvedic physicians in the treatment of this condition is called *vacha*. This herb also grows in marshy land. The rhizome or root of this plant is used in medicine. It is cleaned properly and then made to a fine powder by grinding. One teaspoonful of this powder should be given to the patient twice daily, mixed with honey or cow's ghee. Many Ayurvedic preparations for the promotion of memory like *Sarasvata churna*, contain *brahmi* and *vacha*.

Diet : Food ingredients which are sweet and unctuous are useful in this condition. Cow's milk, cow's ghee and other preparations of cow's milk are advisable. Pungent and spicy food articles, and things having bitter and astringent taste should be avoided. Almond and almond oil are useful in promoting memory. *Amalaki* can be given to the patient in the form of *murabba*, pickles and vegetables.

Other regimens : All the medicines mentioned above act very well when there is mental peace. Therefore all care should be taken to keep the patient free from worries, anxieties, emotional stress and strain. The patient should be advised to follow religious practices and adopt religious prayers. Meditation for some time according to the method prescribed in Yoga serves a very useful purpose in promoting and correcting memory.

HYSTERIA

It is a common form of the emotional reaction in which a patient tends to act out his or her distress in exaggerated and dramatic form. The purpose of hysteria is to attract the attention of the people and gain sympathy. These patients may develop symptoms which have no anatomical or clinical basis. The illness is often precipitated by dramatic events, such as an accident, meeting an unwanted person, separation from the beloved, which the patient considers much worse than what it actually is. Hysterical attacks appear abruptly. The patient becomes excited, noisy and full of complaints, or may remain unduly quiet.

In Ayurveda, this is treated as *unmada*. This is also called *yoshapasmara*. Women outnumber men in this particular disease. Often children are affected by this condition.

The symptoms of hysteria are connected with neurotic or emotional factors. However, physically the patient may suffer from hyper-acidity or heart burn, indigestion, or even an ulcer. They may affect the intestines resulting either in acute form of constipation, or severe diarrhoea, depending upon the response to emotionally charged situation. It may take the form of colitis with the acute ulceration of the intestinal valve. No organ of the body is immune to the psycho-somatic symptoms or diseases and they may manifest themselves in the form of an allergy, skin eruption or other types of organic and physical illness.

Treatment : *Sarpagandha, brahmi, vacha* and *Shankhapushpi* are the drugs of choice for the treatment of this disease. They correct both the body and the mind of the individual. All these drugs are made into a powder and mixed in equal quantities. The patient should take it in a dose of one gm. three times a day, mixed with a cup of milk. These patients usually suffer from sleeplessness or disturbed sleep which is corrected by these medicines. Use of *ashvagandha* gives considerable relief to these patients. A preparation of this drug is known as *Ashvagandharishta*. Six teaspoonfuls of this liquid medicine is given to the patients after food, twice daily, mixed with equal quantity of water.

The above mentioned therapy is to be given to all types of hysterical patients. The other symptoms from which these patients suffer automatically subside, when there is improvement in their neurotic and emotional conditions. Drugs containing cannabis are often used for the treatment of hysteria. For those suffering from chronic colitis, *jatiphaladi churna* is considered to be very useful. One teaspoonful of this powder is to be given to the patient, three times a day, mixed with a cup of buttermilk. This promotes the tranquillity of his mind and relieves him of his colitis.

Diet : Hot and spicy food should be avoided. Fried things and pulses are not good for patients. Almond and almond oil are good for these patients. A patient should be given almond oil in a dose of one teaspoonful, mixed with a cup of milk at bedtime. It strengthens the nervous system. Mangoes, oranges, apples, peaches and bananas are useful in this condition.

Other regimens : The cause for the emotional upset of the patient should be located, and efforts should be made to make him free from it. The patient should be loved and taken care of. He should not be teased, and as far as possible, there should be no mention about the disease before the patient. He should be permitted to have full night's sleep. Walk in the early morning considerably helps the patient to develop his will power which is essential to overcome this disease.

SCHIZOPHRENIA

Schizophrenia is a chronic mental disorder characterised by hallucination and delusion. In Ayurveda it is classified under *unmada.*

Psychic stress and strain are primarily responsible for the causation of this disease. Irregularity in food and constipation often aggravate the condition.

The signs and symptoms vary considerably in different types of schizophrenia. The patient is unable to sleep, talks and acts incoherently, and often becomes violent.

Treatment : *Dhara* is considered to be the best therapy for this condition. Normally *Kshirbala taila* is used in dhara. This oil is kept in an adjusted vessel over the forehead of the patient and the vessel is adjusted in such a way that continuous drops of this medicated oil fall from the bottom of the vessel onto the place between the two eyebrows of the patient. This should be done once daily. By this process the patient sleeps well and recovers from the disease slowly *Jatamansi, vacha* and *sarpagandha* are popularly used for this disease. In powder form, these are given to the patient in a dose of one teaspoonful (separately or in a compound form) three times a day with milk or cold water. This brings about tranquillity of mind.

Vatakulantaka rasa is also used for the treatment of this condition. It is a mercurial preparation which is used in a dose of one tablet three times a day mixed with honey.

Diet : Pulses, beans and fried things should be avoided. Milk, ghee and butter should be given to the patient in sufficiently large quantity. Pungent and astringent things are not useful in this condition. Saffron is very useful.

Other regimens : Since this is primarily a psychic disease, psychotherapy is considered to be the ideal treatment. The patient should be induced to offer prayers and observe religious rites. Meditation serves a very useful purpose in curing these patients. Factors which are responsible for psychic stress and strain should be ascertained and removed.

SCIATICA

This is kind of nervous pain. It is experienced in the region of the buttocks, back of the thigh and the leg served by sciatic nerve. In Ayurveda this is known as *gridhrasi.*

Inflammation in the region where the sciatic nerve passes through the curve of the hip-bone is responsible for this disease.

This is caused by the aggravation of *vayu* and physical strain. Constipation often precipitates or aggravates an attack of this disease.

Apart from the pain which is often excruciating in the hip, backside of the thigh and leg, the patient experiences difficulty in walking, and he may not be able to sleep well.

Treatment: *Eranda* is the drug of choice for the treatment of this condition. It is given in the form of a linctus which is called *Eranda paka.*

This is given to the patient in a dose of two teaspoonfuls at bedtime with a cup of warm water or milk. This is very useful for patients who are constipated because it acts as a laxative. *Guggulu* is popularly used for the treatment of all pains of the nervous system. *Yogaraja guggulu* which contains *guggulu* as an important ingredient is given to the patient in a dose of two tablets four times a day along with warm milk or water. For external application, *saindhavadi taila* is considered to be very useful. It is used for massage on the painful parts specially on the affected buttock from the top down. Hot fomentation by a packet of salt tied up in the form of a round bolus in a piece of linen is very useful. This should be done when the patient is going to bed. After this fomentation, the buttock and leg of the patient should be kept covered with a warm cloth.

Diet : Pulses, beans and fried things are strictly prohibited. The patient should not take curd or any other sour thing, including sour fruit. Saffron is used both as medicine and an ingredient of food in this condition. This should be mixed with warm milk and given to the patient.

Other regimens: Gentle exercise of the leg is useful. Strenuous exercise including running and jumping is prohibited. As far as possible the patient should bathe in hot water and not use cold water in any form. Swimming in moderately cold water is, however, considered to be exceedingly useful.

SLEEPLESSNESS

There are several theories about the factors which are responsible for sleep. Fatigue, the darkness and tranquillity of night and habit are some common factors which cause sleep. A normal healthy individual should sleep for about six hours a day. It is always better for an individual to go to bed early and leave the bed also well before the sunrise. There are others, who because of their professional requirements remain awake at night. They should sleep during day-time for a longer period.

For normal individuals, sleep during the day is prohibited. During the winter it is strictly prohibited. In summer, however, a nap is permitted for a short while during the day. People suffering from indigestion are advised

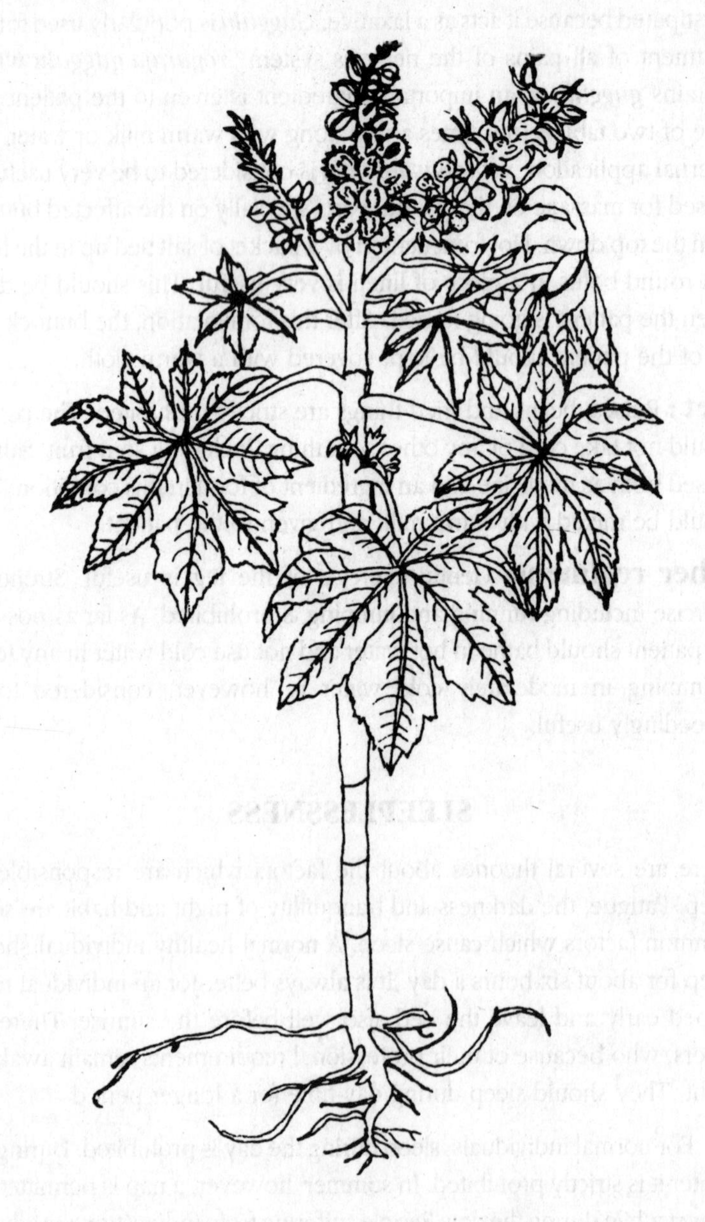

Fig. 16 *Ricinus communis* (*eranda*)

to sleep for about half an hour before taking food, and those suffering from spur syndrome should sleep after eating. Patients suffering from chronic disease and some of the acute ones like fever require more sleep. This helps the promotion of the anabolic aspect of the metabolic system and catabolism is reduced to the minimum.

Among the various age groups, children require more sleep than older people. Those who are exposed to hard physical labour also require more sleep. Mental work also results in fatigue of the brain cells and this leads to sleep. Excessive mental work and less physical work often creates difficulty in sleeping. Normal mental work apart, worry, anxiety, anger, emotional stress and strain causes sleeplessness.

All the factors that are responsible for aggravation of *vayu* and *pitta* in the human body result in sleeplessness. Intake of spicy food, stimulating drinks, exercise immediately after meals, environmental factors like excessive heat, cold or rain, exposure to noise and change of environment along with the psychic factors enumerated above lead to sleeplessness. There are many drugs which when taken for the treatment of some other types of diseases result in sleeplessness. It occurs as a normal physiological phenomenon in ladies during menopause, and men during their old age. There are many diseases like high blood pressure, heart disease, disease of kidney and liver and other conditions associated with pain in different parts of the body which result in sleeplessness.

Insomnia or sleeplessness may be transitory or may continue for a long time. It causes many other troubles. Glands secreting hormones do their work properly and disturbance in sleep affect them considerably which results in the manifestation of diseases. Heart diseases and high blood pressure follow a prolonged period of sleeplessness. During sleep, bad dreams disturb the patient.

Sleeplessness results in weakness and the patient may get constipation, indigestion and wind formation in the stomach.

Treatment: The causes of sleeplessness should be ascertained and removed. If in spite of that, sleeplessness persists, then medicines should be administered. *Brahmi, vacha* and *amalaki* are the drugs of choice for the treatment of this condition. The powder of these three drugs are taken individually or together and given to the patient in a dose of one teaspoon three times a day followed by a cup of ordinary tap water or milk each time. *Til* oil should be boiled with the powder of these drugs and used for massaging the head and body before bathing which gives sound sleep.

The commonly used home remedy for this condition is ripe banana. To this fruit, about a teaspoon of fried powder of cumin seeds is to be added and taken at night before going to bed.

The best therapy for the treatment of sleeplessness, particularly when it becomes chronic is known as *dhara*. For the preparation of this therapy, buffalo milk (about two liters) should be boiled with 60 gms. of the powder of *amalaki*, which is then made into curd. This is then churned by adding water to it and butter removed. The butter-milk should be dripped into the forehead (between two eye-brows) of the patient while lying flat on his back. This should be continued for about 14 to 20 minutes. This is well known for its therapeutic efficacy in curing insomnia.

Diet : Depending upon the digestive power of the patient, he should be given a sufficiently nourishing diet. Heavy food always helps to get good sleep provided the patient has the power to digest the food. Buffalo milk, butter and ghee are considered to be very useful. Hot and spicy food ingredients should be avoided.

Other regimens : Massage and regular bath in cold water is useful. The patient should be made to do physical exercise in addition to mental work. Constipation should be removed. A brisk walk in the evening and early morning is useful. The psychic factors producing stress and strain and factors responsible for anxiety, worry and sorrow should be removed.

CHPATER 11

DISEASES OF DIGESTIVE SYSTEM

AMOEBIC DYSENTERY

In Ayurveda amoebic dysentery is known as *Pravahika*. It is an infection caused by an organism. According to Ayurveda, this organism is only a secondary factor in the causation of this disease. Irregularity of diet, intake of heavy indigestible food and emotional factors like worry, anxiety and anger are mainly responsible for the manifestation of this disease.

This disease is characterised by the passage of mucus along with the stool which occurs frequently and in invariably preceded by gripping pain. There is loss of appetite and the patient feels excessively weak. In chronic amoebic dysentery, the liver is affected seriously and the patient loses a considerable amount of weight.

Treatment: *Kutaja* is the drug of choice for the treatment of this condition. The bark of this plant is given to the patient in powdered form in a dose of one teaspoonful, three times a day. It is also given in the form of a decoction. To prepare this, 30 gms. of the powder of this drug is boiled with two cups of water and reduced to one-fourth. After filtration the decoction should be given to the patient twice daily. Because of its bitterness, some honey may be added while giving it to the patient.

The patient will have frequent motions but the stools containing mucus will be of small quantity. He may even feel constipated. Constipation is extremely bad for these patients. Therefore, as a routine, the patient should be given about two teaspoonfuls of the husk of *Isabagol* at bedtime with milk or butter-milk. In chronic dysentery *Rasaparpati* is popularly used. It is a preparation of mercury and sulphur, and is given to the patient in a dose of 125 gm. three times a day. This should be gradually increased to 250 gm. three times per day. While giving *parpati* therapy, the taking of salt and water should be strictly prohibited. Diet should be limited to milk, boiled rice and sugar.

Diet : The patient should avoid taking fried things. Curd mixed with rice can be given to patient with advantage. *Khichari* or gruel prepared with *moong dal* and rice is very useful in this condition. The patient should not be given spices and chillies. Vegetables and meat should be used as little as possible. Meat and vegetable soups can be given to the patient. Substances having sour and astringent taste like lemon, *amalaki*, pomegranate, banana (both ripe and green) are useful in this condition.

Other regimens : The patient should be given complete bed rest specially in the acute stage of the attack. He should not take bath as far as possible especially during the acute stage of the disease.

CIRRHOSIS OF THE LIVER

The liver is one of the important organs of body in as much as it regulates the digestion, metabolism and many other physiological functions of the body. Damage of this organ may, therefore, lead to chronic gastritis, morning sickness and constipation. Apart from loss of appetite, the patient loses weight because of defective metabolism. He may suffer from diarrhoea and flatulence. There may be a little pain in the right upper portion of the abdomen where the liver is located. Slowly, the size of the liver increases and because of the pressure on diaphragm (the muscular wall which separates the lungs and heart from the organs in the abdomen), the patient suffers from difficulty in breathing and coughing. He may suffer from nausea and vomiting. The liver tissue becomes fibrosed and it shrinks in size. Because of this shrinkage the veinous circulation gets obstructed, and there is accumulation of water in the abdomen.

Treatment: Cirrhosis of liver generally occurs because of faulty diet and excessive intake of alcohol. The liver helps in the neutralisation of the toxic effects of some drugs and beverages like tea and coffee which contain caffeine, and tobacco which contains nicotine. If these toxins are consumed habitually in excess, the liver becomes unable to cope with the demand for neutralising their effects. This results in the cirrhosis of this organ. It is, therefore, desirable in the first instance, to ask the patient to give up these harmful beverages and drinks.

Bhringaraja is the drug of choice for the treatment of this condition. One teaspoonful of the juice of this plant is to be given to a child patient below 8 years of age, three times a day. The taste of the juice of *bhringaraja* is slightly bitter and astringent. Therefore, it is always prescribed to be given to the child with half teaspoonful of honey. This juice will act better if administered on an empty stomach.

Katuki is the drug prescribed by physicians especially when cirrhosis occurs in adults. This herb grows at high altitudes in the Himalayas. The rhizome or the root of this plant is used in the medicine. It is bitter in taste. The powder of this drug in a dose of one teaspoonful is given to an adult patient three times a day mixed with honey in good quantity. If there is constipation then the dose of this powder may be increased to two teaspoonfuls three times a day and it should be given with a cup of warm water each time. This is a cholagogue and acts as a purgative by stimulating the liver to produce more bile. The excretion of this bile in large quantity relieves the congestion in the liver and the tissues which have gone defunct start reviving. A compound preparation called *Arogyavardhini,* contains *katuki*. In addition, this compound preparation contains copper in the form of a *bhasma*. Copper in Ayurveda is considered to be a potent drug to revive the activity of different tissue cells. It is a toxic drug but by a special method of processing, the toxicity of the drug is neutralised and it is easily absorbed into the human system. *Arogyavardhini* is available in the form of a tablet of 0.25 gm. each. Depending upon the seriousness of the disease, two to four tablets of this drug are given to the patient three times a day followed by a cup of warm water each time.

Diet : The patient should not be given any food which is difficult to digest. Oil, ghee and such other fats are to be avoided. Vegetables which are bitter in taste like patola, bitter gourd and bitter variety of drumstick should be given to the patient. Buffalo milk which contains a high percentage of fat is contra-indicated. Goat's milk and cow's milk can be given in small quantity. Camel's milk is considered very useful in this disease especially when, as a complication, there is accumulation of water in the abdomen, which is commonly called 'ascites'. Curd should not be given to the patient but butter-milk prepared by churning the curd (prepared of cow's milk) is exceedingly useful. This should be given to the patient after removing all the fat. Garlic is useful. If there is accumulation of water in the abdomen, the patient should be given salt-free diet. He should be advised to miss a few meals and observe fasting which helps in promoting the function of liver.

Other regimens: The patient should be prohibited from sleeping during daytime and riding a fast moving vehicle on an uneven surface. He should not be exposed to violent jerks and should not resort to any strenuous physical exercise. He should be given rest as far as possible and only walking is permitted.

COLIC PAIN

An acute, paroxysmal abdominal pain is known as colic pain. Depending upon the cause of pain, it is of several types. The common causes of colic are appendicitis, gall-stone, kidney stone, intestinal spasm, duodenal and gastric ulcer and inflammation of the ovary or liver. In Ayurveda, it is known as *shula.* It is mainly caused by the aggravation of *vayu.*

Colic pain may appear all of sudden, or gradually. Digestion and appetite are usually affected. The patient is constipated. The pain might spread to other parts of the body such as the scapular region, or the genital organs. There might be vomiting and nausea. Other signs and symptoms vary depending upon the organ or part of the body affected.

Treatment: In the beginning, efforts are made to remove the constipation which alleviates *vayu.* This can be done by the administration of a mild purgative or a castor oil enema.

Shankha bhasma is the medicine of choice. This is given in a dose of 325 gm. four times a day followed by a cup of hot water. *Mahashankha vati,* which contains *shankha bhasma* as an important ingredient, is generally used by physicians. It is given in a dose of two tablets four times a day with a cup of hot water.

Hing and *lasuna* are also considered to be very useful in this condition. *Hingvashtaka churna*, which contains *hing* as an important ingredient, is used for the treatment of colic pain in a dose of one teaspoonful to be taken with water three times a day. *Lasunadi vati* containing *lasuna* is given in a dose of two tablets four times per day.

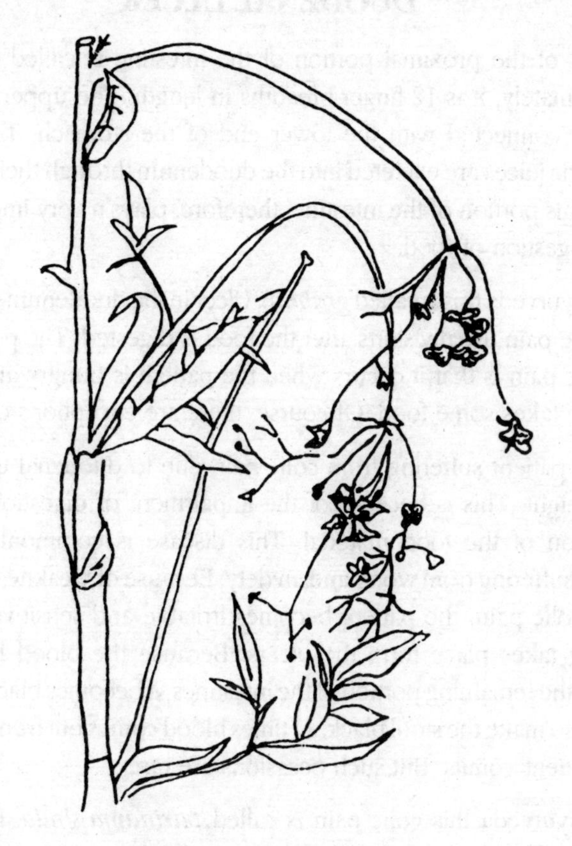

Fig. 17 *Ferula foetida* (*hing*)

Abhraka bhasma is also useful in giving relief to all type of colic pain. It is given in a dose of 250 gm. four times a day mixed with honey.

The organs affected should be treated separately.

Diet : Pulses, beans and fried things are strictly prohibited. The patient should take sufficient rest. Exercise immediately after taking food should be avoided. Mental worry, anxiety and anger are responsible for the aggravation of *vayu,* which is responsible for the causation of this condition. They should therefore be avoided.

DUODENAL ULCER

The first of the proximal portion of the intestine is called duodenum. Approximately, it is 12 finger-breadths in length. The upper end of this organ is connected with the lower end of the stomach. The bile and pancreatic juices are excreted into the duodenum through their respective ducts. This portion of the intestine, therefore, plays a very important role in the digestion of food.

In Ayurveda this is called *grahani.* Ulcer in the duodenum causes colic pain. The pain usually starts after the food is digested. The peculiarity of this colic pain is that it occurs when the patient is hungry and subsides when he takes some food. Of course, there are exceptions of this rule.

The patient suffering from colic pain due to duodenal ulcer slowly loses weight. This is because of the impairment of digestion and non-absorption of the food material. This disease is commonly found in patients suffering from worry and anxiety. Because of weakness produced by the colic pain, the patient becomes irritable and sensitive. At times, bleeding takes place form the ulcers. Because the blood has to pass through the remaining portion of the intestines, it becomes black in colour. It may also make the stool black. At times blood comes out from the mouth if the patient vomits. But such occasions are rare.

In Ayurveda this colic pain is called *parinama shula.* It is caused mainly by the aggravation of *vayu.* Individuals having vatika type of physical constitution and psychic temperament are more prone to get this disease.

Treatment: *Sukumara ghrita* is the medicine of choice for the condition. The most important ingredients of this medicine are ghee and castor oil. This medicated ghee is to be given to the patient in a dose of two teaspoonfuls on an empty stomach mixed with a cup of warm milk. If milk is not agreeable to the patient, then this medicated ghee can be given, mixed well with a cup of hot water. The dose of this ghee is to be gradually increased. At times, the digestive power of the patient is affected by the intake of ghee. In that case the dose of this medicated ghee should be reduced. After taking this medicine for two or three days, the digestive power of the patient improves automatically. Then he becomes capable of taking more and more of this ghee. The dose of this ghee should then be increased at the rate to 1/2 teaspoonful every day. About six teaspoons of ghee can be given to the patient in a gradually increased dosage, and this will not cause any inconvenience or discomfort to the patient though he may feel lazy due to drowsiness and headache.

The medicine commonly used by Ayurvedic physicians for the treatment of any type of colic pain is *shankha bhasma*. Half a teaspoonful of this powder should be given to the patient two to three times a day to be followed by a cup of hot water each time. When the patient is suffering from excruciating pain, then a preparation of *shankha bhasma* known as *Mahashankha vati* is to be given to the patient. It is usually given in a dose of two tablets. two to four times a day depending upon the nature of the pain. After taking this medicine a cup of warm water is to be taken by the patient. This reduces the pain and promotes digestion.

The nature of this disease is such that with a little treatment or even without any treatment it may automatically subside. But it may recur again when there is any disturbance in the intake of food or during psychic stress or strain. For the permanent cure of this disease, the medicated ghee described above is considered to be the best, and it should be taken for a sufficiently long time even after the colic pain is over. There are many other medicated ghee preparations like *Amalaki ghrita* and *Shatavari ghrita* which are also used in the treatment of this condition.

Diet : Articles of food which produce dryness and roughness in the body are contra-indicated in this condition. Pulses of all types and their preparations are also strictly prohibited. The patient should not take fried things. Spices, chillies and sour things are also prohibited.

The patient can be given milk, cheese, ghee, rice, wheat, *amalaki* and pomegranate.

Other regimens: The patient should be kept free from mental stress and strain, and care should be taken to keep him away from worry and anxiety. He should be given sufficient rest and should not be permitted to observe fast or keep an empty stomach for a long time. Care should be taken to see that he gets good sleep for a sufficiently long time. A few hours of sleep during the day time, specially after lunch, may be of help to the patient. He should not suffer from constipation. This may lead to wind-formation in the abdomen which will precipitate or aggravate the attack of pain. If he is found to be constipated then a laxative should be administered. Castor oil is considered to be a good purgative. Husk of *Isabagol* may be given to the patient regularly at bedtime.

FLATULENCE

Distention of the stomach and intestines due to wind is called flatulence. Normally wind is formed during the process of digestion, but is passed out in the form of flatus. If not, or if formed in excess, this leads to distension of the intestine and stomach. In Ayurveda this conditions is called *adhmana*.

Due to distension, the patient experiences discomfort, loss of appetite, indigestion, breathlessness, headache and sleeplessness. It is usually associated with constipation.

Treatment : If constipation is the cause *Hing triguna taila* should be given to the patient in a dose of two teaspoonfuls once a day on an empty stomach with a cup of hot water. *Kumari asava* in a dose of 30 ml. twice daily after food with an equally quantity of water is an ideal medicine.

Hingvashtaka churna should be given to the patient in a dose of one teaspoonful twice daily mixed with one teaspoonful of ghee and followed by hot water.

Diet : Fried things and pulses as well as beans of all types should be avoided. Milk would not be easily digestible to the patient. Curd and butter-milk would be useful.

Other regimens : Any hard labour immediately after taking food is prohibited. The patient should take some rest after food. He should avoid worry and anxiety especially while taking food.

GASTRITIS

Inflammation of the stomach is known as gastritis. It is of several types depending upon the nature of the inflammation, the condition of the mucous membrane and glands. Hydrochloric acid and some other digestive enzymes are secreted by the glands of the stomach. Inflammation of the stomach thus results in the impairment of these secretions leading to indigestion. In Ayurveda, this condition is known as *urdhvaga amlapitta.*

Irregularity in diet, intake of chillies and spices, anger, anxiety and worry specially during the time of taking the food are responsible for the causation of gastritis. Persons having *paittika* type of constitution are prone to get this disease. It is aggravated when the patient suffers from constipation.

The patient experiences acid eructation accompanied by a burning sensation in the chest. The appetite is either suppressed or their is a false appetite. The patient feels weak and irritable. There might be pain in the upper part of the abdomen which is sometimes aggravated immediately after taking food, or even when the stomach is empty. If pressure is exerted there might be tenderness in the upper part of the stomach. The patient may also suffer from nausea, giddiness and headache. Patients suffering from chronic gastritis become emaciated and anaemic.

Treatment : Gastritis or *urdhvaga amlapitta* is caused by vitiation of *pitta.* The best therapy for the correction of *pitta* is purgation. Ghee also plays an important role in alleviating *pitta.* Therefore, medicated ghee, which works as a laxative as well, is useful in the treatment of this condition. Commonly *Sukumara ghrita* is used for the treatment of this condition. It is given in a dose of two teaspoonfuls twice daily mixed with a cup of milk on an empty stomach. In the beginning, this may affect the power of digestion. After a day or two, digestion improves and the patient does not experience any difficulty.

Amalaki is the drug of choice for the condition. It is given to the patient in powder form in a dose of two teaspoonfuls four times a day. *Dhatri lauha* is often used by the physician for its treatment. The chief ingredient of this compound preparation is *lauha bhasma* and it is impregnated with the juice of *amalaki*. This is given to the patient in a dose of one teaspoonful twice daily. If the patient is constipated, *Avipattikara churna* is the medicine of choice. It is given in a dose of two teaspoonfuls at bedtime. The chief ingredient of this medicine is *trivrit*. The root-bark of this drug stimulates the liver and thus works as a laxative. Coconut and white variety of pumpkin are also used as medicine for the treatment of this condition.

Diet : Barley, wheat, rice (preserved for one year), soup of *moong dal*, parched rice, cucumber, bitter gourd, *patola*, green banana, banana flower, white pumpkin, pomegranate and cow's milk are considered to be exceedingly useful for the treatment of this condition. Sesame seeds, *masha, kulattha*, gram, pungent and sour things, heavy food, curd and alcoholic drinks are harmful. The patient should preferably be kept exclusively on milk diet (added with sugar) or on a diet consisting of milk and old rice.

Other regimens : The patient should not expose himself to hard mental or physical work. He should avoid anxiety, worry and anger. He should be given complete rest. A walk in the early morning for about a mile is very useful.

HEMATEMESIS

Vomiting of blood is called hematemesis. It is not a disease by itself but is a sign of some other diseases of the gastrointestinal tract. In Ayurveda it is called *rakta vami* and it belongs to the group of conditions called *rakta pitta*. Gastric ulcer, gastric cancer, chronic gastritis are some of the diseases in which blood vomiting takes place. The blood vomited is mixed with food particles, mucus or water. It might also come out in the vomit alone.

Treatment : *Amalaki* is the drug of choice for this condition. The juice of the fruit of this drug is given to the patient in a dose of 30 ml. three times a day. The juice of *Kushmanda* can similarly be given in a dose of 30 ml. three times a day. *Pravala pishti* (a preparation of coral) is helpful in the treatment. It is given to the patient in a dose of one gm. three times per day, mixed with honey. For immediate stoppage of bleeding, iced water can be given to the patient to drink.

Diet: Old rice, *moong dal* and *patola* are given to the patient. Pomegranate, *amalaki*, banana (both ripe and unripe), milk, ghee and butter are useful in this condition. Hot and spicy things should be avoided.

Other regimens: The patient should be given complete rest and should not expose himself to sun.

INDIGESTION

Indigestion is not a disease by itself. It is a symptom of many other diseases. It might be caused because of some disturbances in the intestine or stomach. It might also be caused by some diseases in other parts of the body, Even without a disease one may suffer from indigestion by overeating or eating wrong food in a wrong manner. It may result in a feeling of heaviness in the stomach, pain, vomiting, diarrhoea, nausea, acid eructation and burning sensation in the chest.

In Ayurveda this condition is called *agnimandya*. It is caused by the aggravation of *doshas*, viz., *vata, pitta* and *kapha*. Characteristic symptoms of *agnimandya* caused by the vitiation of these *doshas* are elaborately described in Ayurvedic texts. In brief, when *vata* is vitiated there is more pain, when *pitta* is vitiated there is more of burning sensation, and when *kapha* is vitiated there is more of *nausea* and vomiting.

Psychic factors like anger, anxiety and worry play an important role in the digestion of food. According to Ayurveda the food taken in time and in proper quantity does not get digested if the individual is suffering from these mental afflictions.

About the manner of intake of food, various rules have been prescribed in Ayurvedic classics. For example, one should take food when it is fresh after preparation and when it is hot. One should take such food articles which are unctuous. One should take food articles in proper quantity. Food should be taken after the digestion of the previous meal. Mutually contradictory food articles should not be taken. Food should be taken in pleasant surroundings; it should not be taken in a hurry nor very slowly. While taking food one should not talk a lot, nor laugh. One should carefully examine the food for its suitability and take it without any diversion of mind.

How to know if the previous meal is already digested? In that case the individual gets eructations which are free from any smell. There is proper excretion of stool and urine, one feels lightness in the body and there is normal hunger and thirst.

The quantity and quality of food to be taken varies from season to season and individual to individual. In winter season one should take food articles which are unctuous, sour and saline in taste. Meat of aquatic animals and animals inhabiting marshy land may be used in food. Milk preparations, oil and freshly harvested rice, can be safely consumed. On the other hand in summer season the individual should be given cooling drinks, ghee, milk rice and meat of animals dwelling in forests. He should not be given wine. If there is a necessity for taking wine it should be diluted with sufficient quantity of water.

If the above mentioned rules of taking food are not observed, then the patient may suffer from indigestion.

Treatment : The patient suffering from chronic indigestion can be successfully treated with some home remedies. Five minutes before taking food he should take a piece of raw ginger (of about one gm. of weight) and a piece of rock-salt. Both these should be chewed thoroughly. This promotes appetite and corrects chronic indigestion. For both chronic and acute types of indigestion *Hingvashtaka churna* is popularly used by the Ayurvedic physicians. An important ingredient of this recipes is *hing*. Besides, *shunthi, pippali, maricha, ajmoda, jiraka* and *krishna jiraka* are used in the preparation of this medicine.

This medicine is used in the form of powder. To get the best effect of this medicine, it is given to the patient mixed with the first morsel of food. One teaspoonful of this is given to the patient twice daily mixed with one teaspoonful of ghee. This powder can also be given to the patient after the intake of food in the same dose. Mixing it with butter-milk produces very good results. When indigestion is associated with pain, then *mahashankha vati* is given in a dose of two tablets three or four times a day, followed by a cup of warm water each time.

Diet : The patient should be given a light diet. It is better to observe fast. Instead of taking any solid food the patient may be given a glass of lemon juice to which salt has been added. Garlic serves a very useful purpose for correcting chronic indigestion. Butter-milk is the diet of choice. For the treatment of all types of indigestion, it should be thin and free from fat. Asafoetida in powder form is also useful in this condition.

Other regimens : Sleep after lunch during daytime produces indigestion, and sleep before lunch during daytime helps in digestion. This principle should be kept in view while treating the patient. In acute phases of indigestion the patient should be given physical and mental rest, but in chronic indigestion, the patient should be asked to take physical exercise. He should not be kept awake at night. The patient should be kept free from worries and anxieties.

INFANTILE DIARRHOEA

Intake of defective milk or infection in the alimentary tract causes diarrhoea in children. If the child is fed on the breast milk, the digestive conditions of the mother also affect the digestion of the milk by the child. Along with diarrhoea, the child may even get vomiting and gripping pain in the stomach. The stool may be liquid and foul-smelling, and it may be of greenish or yellowish colour. Diarrhoea is a common manifestation during the teething time of the child.

Treatment : Many brands of gripe waters are available in the market which are commonly used by mothers during such troubles. Most of them contain carminatives, and are harmful, if used for a prolonged period. The commonly used medicine in Ayurveda for this condition is *musta*. This is a small herb which grows in grass fields and hedge rows. The root or rhizome which looks like a small tuber is used as medicine. This should

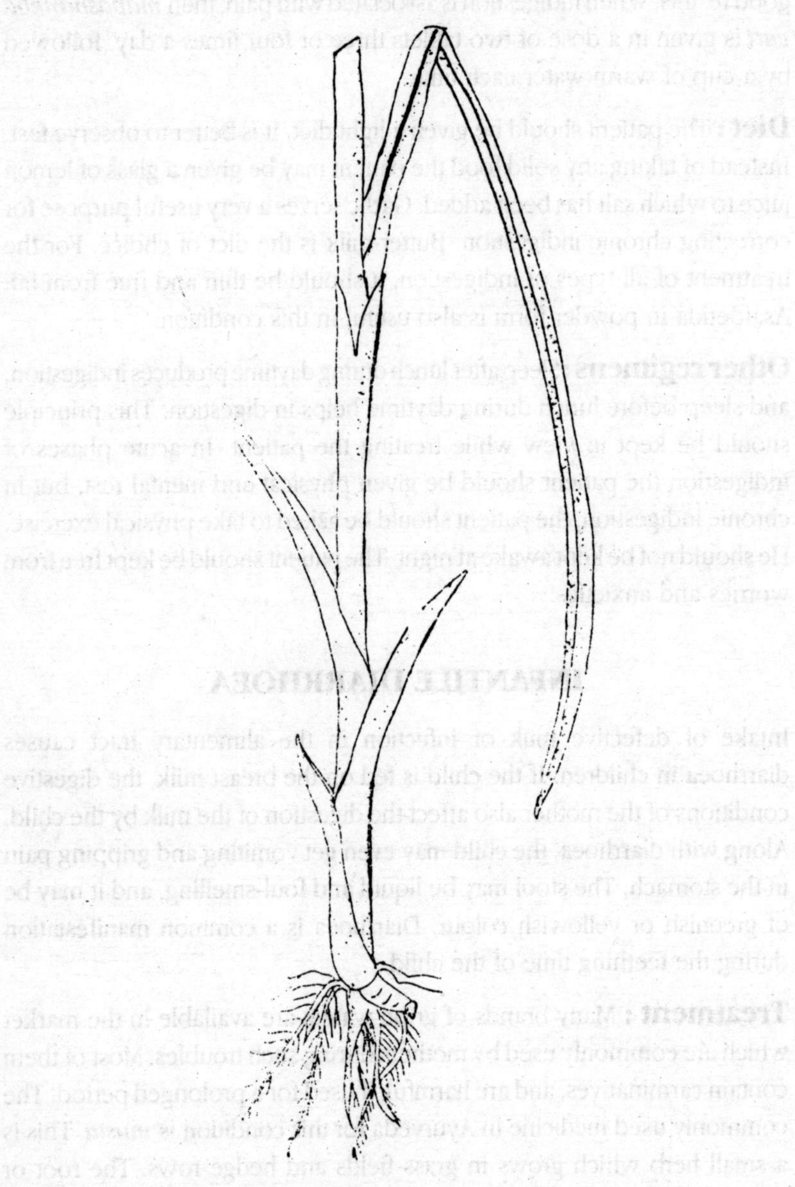

Fig. 18 *Cyperus rotundus* (*musta*)

be cleaned properly and rubbed on a piece of clean stone and made into the consistency of a paste. About 125 gm. of this paste are given to the child three to four times a day. This rhizome may also be used in the form of a powder. 65 gm. of this powder may be given to the child four times a day, mixed with half a teaspoonful of honey each time. This works as a carminative as well. If there are many liquid motions or vomiting then he should be given *jatiphala.* 65 gm. of powder of this seed is given to the child four times a day, mixed with honey. Depending upon the seriousness of the ailment the dose of this drug can be increased.

A compound preparation called *Gorochanadi vatika* is very useful in the treatment of this condition especially when due to frequent, loose motions, the child becomes dehydrated and emaciated. This is available in the form of pills about 30 gm. each. One pill of this drug should be given to the child four times a day, mixed with honey.

Diet : The child should not be given milk containing a high percentage of fat. Cow's milk is normally considered to be good because it contains less fat than buffalo milk. If the child is unable to digest even cow's milk, then goat's milk can be given. Even cow's milk can be given, diluted with water. While boiling the milk, about 125 gm. of the powder of the rhizome of *musta* should be added. If the mother is suffering from indigestion, she should also be treated if she is feeding the child. According to Ayurveda the breast milk of the mother or the wet-nurse gets vitiated by *vayu, pitta* and *kapha*. Characteristic features of the milk that is vitiated by these *doshas* are described in detail in Ayurvedic classics. Such vitiated milk produces many diseases in the child. Therefore, in the first instance the milk of the mother or the wet nurse should be examined and corrected.

When the mother who feeds her child becomes pregnant, lactation slowly stops. But in some cases lactation continues even after pregnancy. If the child takes the milk of the pregnant mother then this causes a diseases which in Ayurveda is known as *parigarbhika.* One of the notable symptoms of this disease is the commencement of diarrhoea. In that case the child should be immediately switched over to some other food.

Other regimens : The child should not be disturbed or teased. It should be permitted to sleep comfortably and as long as it likes. Any disturbances in sleep may causes diarrhoea and vomiting. Long journeys by train or car should be avoided during diarrhoea.

PILES

At times the veins in the anal region, both external and internal, get varicosed and this gives rise to the piles. In Ayurveda this is called *arshas.* Chronic constipation, sitting on hard seats, sitting constantly for long time, lack of exercise and morbidity of the liver are responsible for piles.

Piles are classified into two groups, namely, bleeding piles and dry piles. At times there is so much bleeding that the patient becomes anaemic. Loss of appetite, itching of the anus, wind formation in stomach and lumbago are often associated with this disease.

Treatment : *Nagakesara* is the drug of choice for this condition, specially when it is associated with bleeding. The powder of this flower is given to the patient in a dose of one teaspoonful three times a day. For patient suffering from both dry and bleeding piles, *haritaki* is exceedingly useful. It is given to the patient in powder form in a dose of one teaspoonful two to three times a day followed by milk.

Abhayarishta in which *haritaki* is added predominantly is useful for this condition. It is given to the patient in a dose of 30 ml. twice daily after food with an equal quantity of water. *Kasisadi taila,* of which *kasisa* or iron sulphate is the important ingredient, is used externally. It shrinks the piles and cures itching in the anal region. It relieves pain and checks bleeding.

Diet : *Kulattha,* barley, wheat, old rice, papaya, *amalaki, patola,* and goat's milk are very useful in this condition. The rhizome of *surana* is also exceedingly useful. It is given to the patient in the form of both diet and medicine. Vegetables like potato, yellow variety of pumpkin and colocasia are not advised.

Other regimens : The patient should not suppress natural urges and should not indulge in sex in excess. Riding on the back of animals, and sitting on hard seats are very harmful for the patient.

SPRUE SYNDROME

This is a chronic disease characterised by diarrhoea with frothy stools, indigestion, sore mouth, loss of weight and anaemia. The stool is accompanied by mucus. The patient usually passes a large quantity of stool in the early morning after he gets up from the bed.

In Ayurveda this condition is called *grahani roga*. Like dysentery, it is associated with a gripping pain in the stomach. The small intestine beginning from the duodenum up to the colon is known in Ayurveda as *grahani*. Organisms do not play any significant role in the causation of this disease. It is caused by impairment of the functioning of the inner wall of the small intestine. Sometimes the large intestine is also involved.

According to Ayurveda persons having *paittika* type of physical constitution and psychic temperament are more prone to get this disease. Anger, worry, anxiety and other types of emotional stresses and strains are primarily responsible for the causation of this disease. Irregularity in the intake of food also precipitates the attack of this disease. Impairment of digestion and absorption of food articles results in malnutrition. The tissue elements in the body do not get proper nourishment. The patient becomes emaciated and anaemic. Even the best of nourishing food does not help in this condition.

Treatment : This is a very chronic condition and the patient has to be tackled very carefully. *Rasa parpati* is the drug of choice for the treatment of this condition. The ingredients of this medicine are mercury and sulphur. Both these ingredients have toxic effects upon the body. Therefore, they are processed through a special pharmaceutical method to make them non-toxic and useful for the body.

This *Parpati* is administered to the patient in gradually increased doses. It is to be started with 125 gm. and increased by 65 gm. each day till 625 gms. At this stage the dose is to be maintained for ten days and then gradually reduced by 65 gm. till it reaches 125 gm. again, after which the therapy is to be discontinued. This particular way of giving medicine is called *parpati kalpa*.

During *parpati kalpa* the patient is strictly prohibited from taking salt or water. He is not permitted even to take bath or use water even for sanitary purposes. He is to be given only milk or butter-milk. Sugar can be added to this. In the beginning the patient may feel a little uncomfortable in taking milk only. Subsequently he gets habituated to this. He develops the power to digest large quantities of milk. It is seen that patients who were unable to digest or tolerate even 250 ml. of milk per day, managed to digest about ten to fifteen liters of milk per day after this therapy. This serves as a rejuvenation therapy for the patient. Along with the improvement in the condition of the functioning of the inner wall of the intestine, more and more food ingredients get digested and he picks up weight. Since this involves many diet restrictions it is always advisable to administer this therapy under the supervision of an expert ayurvedic physician.

Jatiphala or nutmeg is the other medicine of choice in this condition. The kernel of the fruit, crushed into powder, may be given three or four times a day depending on the number of motions. There is a recipe called *Jatiphaladi churna* in which nutmeg is added as an important ingredient. One teaspoonful of this powder is given to the patient two to three times a day.

Diet : Fried, oily and spicy food ingredients are strictly contra-indicated in this condition. The patient should be given butter-milk in sufficient quantity. Keeping the patient on buttermilk alone expedites recovery from this disease. Fried cuminseed in the form of powder and rock-salt can be added to this butter-milk according to the taste of the patient. Butter-milk mixed with rice and a little salt form a very good food for the patient. dry fruits are not normally indicated for the patient . Meat and fish are also contra-indicated. Among vegetables, the patient can take green banana, the flower of banana, drumstick, *patola, karavellaka,* tomato and white variety of pumpkin. Yellow variety of pumpkin, colocasia, potato, lady's finger and leafy vegetable are not indicated in this condition. Pomegranate can be given to the patient in various forms.

Other regimens : Even though the patient suffers from diarrhoea, he may at times, get constipation also. In some cases diarrhoea and constipation follow one after the other. The husk of *Isabagol* may be given to the patient in a dose of one to two teaspoonfuls at bedtime, mixed with butter-milk. The patient should be given sufficient rest. He is advised to sleep for one hour during the day. Efforts should be made so that the patient gets good sleep at night. Light exercise or morning walk is very useful in this condition. Over exertion, mental worry, anxiety, anger etc., should be avoided.

THIRST

When there is a demand for water in the body, the person feels thirsty. When the desire for water is excessive it is treated as a disease. In Ayurveda this is called *trishna roga.* Depending upon the *doshas* involved and the pathogenesis of this disease, it is of seven types. In *vatika* type, the patient feels pain and giddiness in addition to thirst. In *paittika* type there is a feelings of burning sensation. In *kaphaja* type, saline taste appears in the mouth.

Treatment : The water from green coconut fruit is exceedingly useful in this condition. It can be given to the patient in any quantity he desires. A piece of brick should be heated and immersed in a vessel containing water. This water should, thereafter, be filtered and given to the patient to drink. This helps to relieve thirst. The juice of ripe tamarind should be made into a syrup by adding sugar, and then boiling it. This should be given to the patient in a dose of 30 ml. four times a day. Green mango should be burnt over the fire and when the outer cover becomes charred, it should be removed from the fire and cooled. The inner pulp of the fruit should then be made into a drink by adding sugar and water. This drink is very effective in relieving thirst. It is also very useful in curing heat stroke.

Diet : Thin gruel prepared of parched rice, juice of *moong dal,* the flower of banana, pomegranate, *amalaki* and *kushmanda* are very useful in this condition. Hot and spicy things should be avoided.

Other regimens : The patient should not be exposed to heat and sun. He should be given rest.

VOMITING

Forcible ejection of the stomach through the mouth is called vomiting. In Ayurveda, it is called *chhardi*. There are several causative factors which include mental worries, intestinal worms, pregnancy and intake of disagreeable or contaminated foodstuff.

In Ayurveda this disease is classified into five categories, namely, *vataja, pittaja, kaphaja, tridoshaja,* and *dvishtratha samyogaja*. *Vataja* type of vomiting is characterised by dryness of mouth, pain in chest and astringent taste in mouth. In *pittaja* type of vomiting, there is burning sensation and sour eructation. In *kaphaja* type of vomiting, there is slime in the vomited material. In *tridoshaja* type of vomiting, signs and symptoms of all the above mentioned three types appear. The fifth type is caused by food poisoning and there is always nausea and a foul smell from the mouth.

Treatment : The peacock feather is very effective in checking all type of vomiting. After burning it over a fire the ash can be given to the patient in a dose of 0.125 gm. four times a day, mixed with honey. The juice of the unripe fruit of *kapittha* mixed with honey and long pepper may be given to the patient in a dose of one teaspoonful four times a day. A small amount of cardamom is very useful in this condition.

Diet : Parched rice is considered both food and a medicine for this condition. It is made into a paste, strained through a linen cloth and diluted in water or butter-milk and administered to the patient. Salt or sugar may be added to this, according to taste. It becomes very effective when given along with the powder of the seeds of green cardamom and clove, about 0.325 gm. of each. Vegetable soup and *badara* fruit are very useful for the patient. The juice of pomegranate can also be given. The patient should not take any solid food during attacks of vomiting.

Other regimens: The patient should be given complete rest and care should be taken to see that he does not become dehydrated.

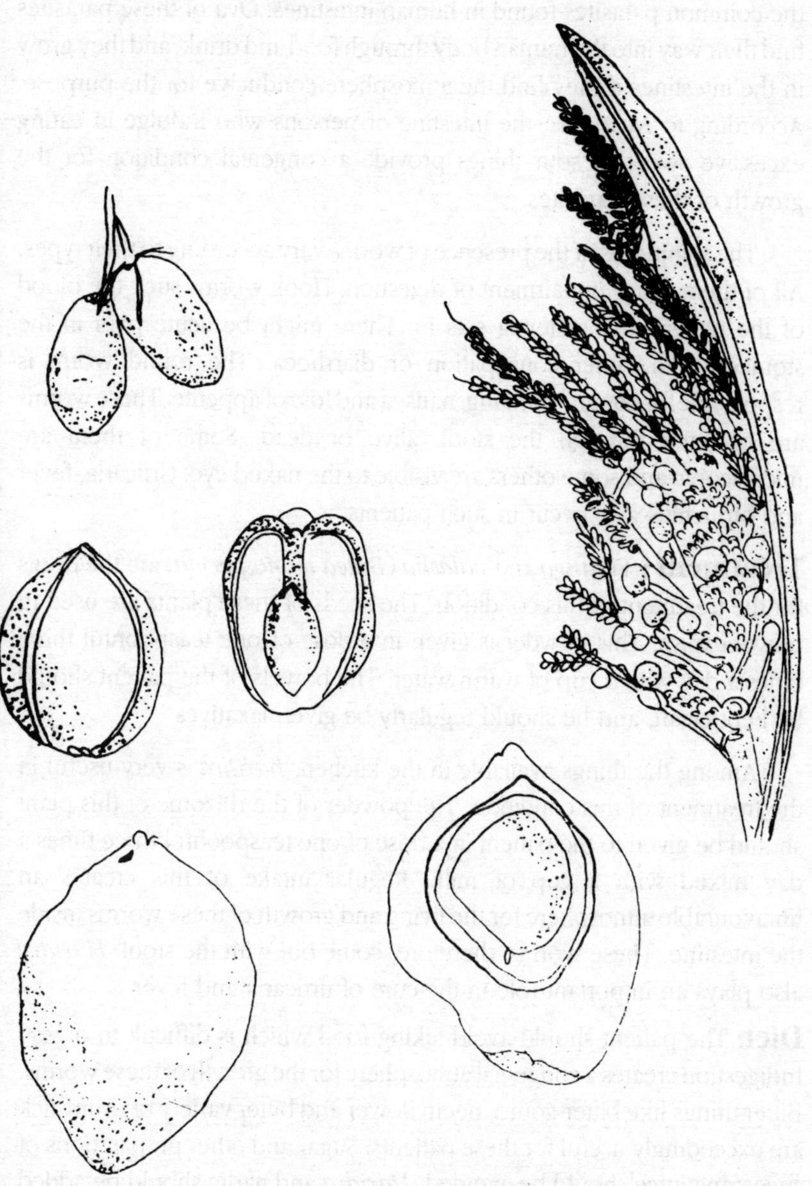

Fig. 19 *Cocos nucifera* (*narikela*)

INTESTINAL WORMS

Round worms, tape worms, hook worms, thread worms and giardia are the common parasites found in human intestines. Ova of these parasites find their way into the human body through food and drink, and they grow in the intestines if they find the atmosphere conducive for the purpose. According to Ayurveda, the intestine of persons who indulge in eating excessive sweet or sour things provide a congenial condition for the growth of these parasites.

The symptoms of the presence of worms vary according to their types. All of them cause impairment of digestion. Hook worms suck the blood of the patient and anaemia sets in. There might be acute pain in the stomach with either constipation or diarrhoea. The round worm is responsible for cough, vomiting, nausea and loss of appetite. These worms are excreted through the stool, alive or dead. Some of them are microscopic and some others are visible to the naked eye. Urticaria, fever and bronchitis also occur in such patients.

Treatment : *Vidanga* and *palasha* (*Butea monosperma*) are the drugs for the treatment of this condition. The seeds of these plants are used in powder form. This powder is given in a dose of one teaspoonful three times a day with a cup of warm water. The bowels of the patient should be kept clean, and he should regularly be given laxatives.

Among the things available in the kitchen, *haridra* is very useful in the treatment of this condition. The powder of the rhizome of this plant should be given to the patient in a dose of one teaspoonful three times a day mixed with a cup of milk. Regular intake of this creates an unfavourable atmosphere for the living and growth of these worms inside the intestine. These worms, therefore, come out with the stool. *Haridra* also plays an important role in the cure of urticaria and fever.

Diet: The patient should avoid taking food which is difficult to digest. Indigestion creates a congenial atmosphere for the growth of these worms. Bitter things like bitter gourd, neem flower and bitter variety of drumstick are exceedingly useful for these patients. Sugar and other preparations of sugarcane juice should be avoided. *Haridra* and garlic should be added to all vegetable preparations in sufficiently large quantities.

Other regimens : Observation of a day's fast every week is very useful for both the prevention and cure of intestinal worms. The patient should never suppress the urge for defecation. He should keep his bowels always clean.

CHRONIC CONSTIPATION

One should pass stools twice a day — once after getting up from bed and once in the evening. This is more essential for vegetarians because their food contains lot of roughage. Some people, however, evacuate their bowels only once in a day, usually in early morning. For them it is normal. They do not suffer from any discomfort because of the non-movement of bowels for the second time. This habit is commonly found amongst city-dwellers whose evening programmes are uncertain. The roughage content of those who take non-vegetarian diet is so little that they do not feel any discomfort even if it remains inside the intestines for 24 hours or more. In European countries where people live mostly on meat, they pass stools once in three or four days, and they consider it normal.

Apart from the roughage from food, stool contains some metabolic waste products. They come out from the blood. Therefore, even if a man does not take anything, he has to pass stools, because the metabolic process that is going on in his body yields some waste products which are to be eliminated only through stools. If they are not eliminated, they cause lot of discomfort locally in the abdomen. There is wind formation, heaviness in the stomach, and loss of appetite. It may also result in headache, sleeplessness and even high blood pressure. Some diseases like asthma, bronchitis, chronic cold and tonsillitis are associated with constipation and once the constipation is removed, the disease automatically disappears. It is therefore, necessary to take care of constipation well in time.

Chronic constipation may be caused by (a) poor bowel habits, improper eating habits, irritable colon, spastic colitis or emotional disturbances; or (b) paralytic or mechanical obstruction to the passage of stools. Such things as adhesions, tumours of the bowel, suture of the anus, or rectum, or inflammatory conditions may produce organic constipation.

Treatment: *Triphala* powder is very popularly used by Ayurvedic physicians for the treatment of chronic constipation. It contains three drugs, namely, *haritaki, bibhitaki* and *amalaki.* Of these three drugs, *haritaki* alone works as a purgative. But while manifesting its action, it produces some adverse effects like gripping pain and wind formation in the stomach. To prevent the adverse effects of this drug and to make it more useful as a tonic, the remaining two drugs are added. *Haritaki* taken alone works as a strong purgative in the beginning, but as days pass by, it does not produce that purgative effect. When added with the remaining two medicines, the purgative effect of this drug continues for a prolonged period. Thereafter, even if purgative effect of this drug is not manifested, it is useful to the patients suffering from constipation because it indirectly helps the bowels to move by stimulating the liver.

Triphala powder is used in two different ways. One or two teaspoonfuls of this are mixed with a cup of warm milk, and some sugar is added to it. The whole thing is taken hot at bedtime. It does not cause any motion during night and its purgative effect is manifested only in the early morning. In the case of persons having chronic constipation and simultaneously a costive bowel, the powder alone does not help. It is to be taken in the form of a decoction. The decoction is prepared by boiling 20 gm. of the powder in 16 times of water and reducing it to one-fourth. Then the powder is to be filtered and the liquid is to be given to the patient.

For those having laxed bowel, *triphala* is used in a different manner. In a glass of water, one teaspoonful of *triphala* powder is soaked overnight. In the morning, it is filtered with a clean cloth. The liquid is taken internally. It is a little astringent in taste and may not be liked by children and people having tender habits. It is, therefore, necessary to add about 2-4 teaspoons of honey with a view to make the potion sweet in taste. Processing of *triphala* in this way is called *Shita kashaya.*

There are many other medicines which help in removing chronic constipation by strengthening the intestinal valves and their functions. They also cure inflammatory conditions of the intestine. One such drug is known as *Agastya rasayana.* Two teaspoonfuls of this drug should be taken regularly, twice a day with any hot drink of choice. Slowly it relieves the individual of his constipative tendency. As the very name indicates, it is also an excellent tonic.

Diet : The patient suffering from chronic constipation should be advised to take fruits, leafy vegetables and fruit juice in plenty. Wheat is better than rice. The bran of both rice and wheat are useful in relieving constipation. The patient should, therefore, use whole meal flour and not refined flour. Similarly, he should use rice along with its bran, and not polished rice. Among the vegetable, *surana* and *papaya* are very useful in relieving constipation. Fried things, pulses and preparations of pulses are extremely harmful for patients suffering from chronic constipation. There are some vegetables which work in both ways — spinach relieves constipation of patients and it also produces constipation tendency in some patients who are suffering from chronic diahorrea. Same is true about banana and *papaya.* Taking sugarcane juice is very useful for relieving constipation.

Other regimens: Regularity in the habit of evacuating bowels is very important for a person to keep himself free from chronic constipation. Whether he gets motion or not, he should attend to the call of nature. Persons who are given to sedentary activities are often exposed to constipation and constipation produces several other diseases like fistula and piles in them. It is, therefore, necessary that persons suffering from chronic constipation should undertake some physical exercises regularly. Walking a few kilometers is also sufficient for a person to get himself relieved of his constipation. Excessive intake of tea and coffee is harmful for such person. Mental worries and anxieties have a great role to play in causing constipation. It is, therefore, necessary that the patient should change his daily habits and lead a care-free life to keep himself free from this ailment.

CHAPTER 12

METABOLIC, GLANDULAR AND JOINT DISEASES

CERVICAL SPONDYLOSIS

A specific form of arthritis which attacks vertebrae and connecting bony and ligamental structures, is known as spondylitis. It is of three types. The osteo-arthritic type of spondylitis is known as spondylosis. Frequently it occurs in the cervical vertebrae. The spines of majority of people above the age of 50 have certain degree of osteo-arthritic changes. But they seldom cause acute symptoms. Certain precipitating factors like trauma, incorrect posture of the body, pressure while sleeping and excessive intake of sour food, usually precipitate these attacks. In Ayurveda this condition is known as *griva sandhigata vata.*

Pain in the back of neck, shoulder and arms, stiffness of the neck and even paraplegia occur due to this condition. The pain of the neck is generally aggravated by the movement of the spine. It is often associated with loss of memory and sleeplessness.

Treatment : Any external massage is not of much use. Violent massage with deep pressure is very harmful for the patient. Only gentle massage over the muscles of the neck and shoulder joints should be applied and for this purpose *Mahanarayana taila* is best suited. This gentle massage can be given 2-3 times a day. In winter season, this medicated oil should be gently warmed before application.

Guggulu, gum-resin extracted from the plant is the best medicine for the treatment of this condition. A compound preparation named as *Simhanada guggulu* is popularly used by ayurvedic physicians for the treatment of this condition. It is given in a dose of 2-4 tablets, four times a day. Usually hot water or hot milk is given to the patient after the administration of this medicine. This medicine has a slightly laxative effect. For the patient to recover from this ailment, it is necessary that his bowels should move clearly and regularly. This medicine is very helpful for this purpose. For patients having clear motions, this medicine should be given in a dose of 2 tablets and for constipated patients the dose should be 4 tablets. If the constipation is not relieved even by taking 4 tablets, the dose can be further increased to 6 tablets.

At night some medicine should be given to the patient which will act as a purgative. *Triphala* powder is the best medicine for this purpose. One teaspoonful of *triphala* should be given to the patient, mixed with a cup of warm milk and one spoon of sugar. If the motions become regular by the intake of *Simhanada guggulu,* then *triphala* powder should be given only twice a week; otherwise it can be given every day.

Hot fomentation on the vertebrae of the neck is very useful for this condition. In a big handkerchief about 500 gm. of salt should be kept over a frying pan till it becomes tolerably hot. Then this should be applied over the neck. Care should be taken to see that it not too hot. In that case, it may cause burns. Sometimes patients suffering from cervical spondylosis develop some anaesthetic patches in the back, neck, shoulders and arms, because of the pressure from nervous system. The patient is, therefore, not able to feel the quantum of heat applied during fomentation. It should, therefore, be the responsibility of the attendant to examine the heat of the bolus before applying it on the affected parts. This fomentation should be continued for about half an hour every day. After fomentation, the affected part should not be exposed to cold wind. In winter season, therefore, immediately after fomentation, the affected part should be covered with some woollen garment. In other seasons also, the affected part should be kept covered with some cotton garments after fomentation. It is very convenient to take the fomentation before bedtime. After the fomentation the patient should go to sleep so that he does not run the risk of exposure.

Diet : Sour things, particularly curd, are strictly prohibited. Fried things, pulses and various preparations of pulses are also contra-indicated in this condition. Bitter vegetables like bitter variety of drumstick, *neem* flowers and bitter gourd are very useful. Wheat is better than rice for the patient. He should, however, avoid taking refined wheat which is known as *maida* (flour) and *suji* (semolina). To some extent they are constipative and do not help the patient in his recovery.

Other regimens : Exposure to cold, cold bath and any violent exercise of the neck muscles, including pressure, are very bad for the patients. Under the impression that this pain is being caused by some defects in the muscles, people undertake different types of exercise of the neck. While reading and writing, one should maintain a comfortable posture. The ratio between the height of the table and the chair should be correct, so that the patient while reading or writing, does not bend too much to put any pressure on his neck muscles. If the pain is acute even ordinary head bath is prohibited. Morning walk gives considerable relief to the patient; but if it is cold outside, the patient should always use a woollen scarf around his neck while going out of the house.

DIABETES

Diabetes is of two types, viz., diabetes mellitus and diabetes insipidus. In the former type, the blood sugar level goes up and sugar appears in the urine. This condition is commonly called diabetes. Because of the impairment of sugar metabolism, the tissue cells do not get enough material for the production of energy, and this results in weakness of the patients. Higher blood sugar level leads to many other complications like coma and carbuncles.

This disease is known as *madhumeha* in Ayurveda. This is called a "rich man's disease" because people who are overnourished usually get afflicted by it. It is characterised by excessive hunger, thirst, urination and weakness. It may cause a burning sensation on the soles of the feet. This type of diabetes which occurs in small children is called juvenile diabetes. It is difficult to cure. In diabetes insipidus, there is excessive urination but the urine is free from sugar. This condition is not so difficult to cure.

Treatment : While treating such cases, efforts are made to reduce the body fat of the patient, and regulate the function of the gland called pancreas with a view to promoting sugar metabolism. *Karela* (bitter gourd) is effectively used in this condition. This is a vegetable, and the juice of the leaves and fruits of the plant is used in a dose of 30 ml. twice daily, preferably on an empty stomach.

Shilajatu or mineral pitch is another medicine which is highly recommended for treatment of diabetes. *Vasanta kusumakara* is another drug for the treatment of diabetes. It is given in a dose of 0.125 gm. twice daily on an empty stomach mixed with cream (half teaspoon) and sugar (one fourth of a teaspoon.)

In an advanced stage, and if not attended to in time, diabetes may produce many complications like coma and carbuncles. For this, it is necessary to immediately reduce the blood sugar, and treatment should be taken under the direct supervision of an expert ayurvedic physician.

Diet : Sugar in any form, rice, potato, banana, and such other cereals and fruits which contain high percentage of carbohydrates are contra-indicated. Similarly, fats should be avoided. There should be control over the quantity of diet. Vegetable like *Karela* (bitter gourd), fruits and leaves of drumstick, *patola* and *bimbi* are specially useful in this condition. All bitter things, in general, are good for this disease. Vegetables prepared of neem flower and neem leaves are extremely good. It has been reported that regular intake of two tender leaves each of *neem* and *bilva* in the morning considerably reduces blood sugar.

Other regimens : Sleep during the daytime is strictly prohibited. The patient should resort to moderate exercise. Yogic exercise, specially *paschimottanasana* is very useful. The patient should take care not to cut or injure himself, because in diabetes, the healing process is very slow as a result of which there is every possibility of the wound becoming septic. If the patient is attacked by any other disease then it should be attended to immediately because the patient of this disease usually lacks resistance, and the disease is very likely to take an acute turn if not treated early.

GOITRE

This disease is characterised by the enlargement of the thyroid gland resulting in a swelling in the front part of the neck. Depending upon the nature of morbidity it is divided into several types. In Ayurveda this is called *galaganda*.

It is usually manifested because of lack of iodine in food and drink. According to Ayurveda this is caused by the aggravation of *kapha* and diminution of *pitta*.

The swelling of the gland in the neck becomes visible and the gland at times becomes exceedingly large, thereby causing difficulty in respiration and swallowing of foods and drinks.

Treatment: *Kanchanara* is the drug of choice for the treatment of this condition. The bark of this tree is given to the patient in the form of a decoction. It is administered in a dose of 30 ml. twice daily on an empty stomach. *Kanchanara guggula*, which contains this drug as an important ingredient, is popularly used for the treatment of this disease. It is given in a dose of four tablets three times a day followed by milk or warm water.

Diet: Old rice, barley, *moong dal, patola*, drumstick, cucumber, sugarcane, juice, milk and milk products are useful in this conditions. Sour and heavy articles of food are contra-indicated.

Other regimens : Exercise of the neck is useful in this condition.

GOUT

This is painful metabolic disease resulting in inflammation and chalky deposits in the joints due to disturbance of the purine metabolism in the body. In Ayurveda this is known as *vatarakta*, Impairment of digestion and metabolism because of the intake of mutually contradictory food articles and non-elimination of the metabolic waste products from the body are responsible for the causation of this disease.

The characteristic features of this disease are the involvement of the big toe in the beginning which becomes acutely painful and swollen. Gradually, other joints are involved and the patient experiences difficulty in walking, talking and even moving.

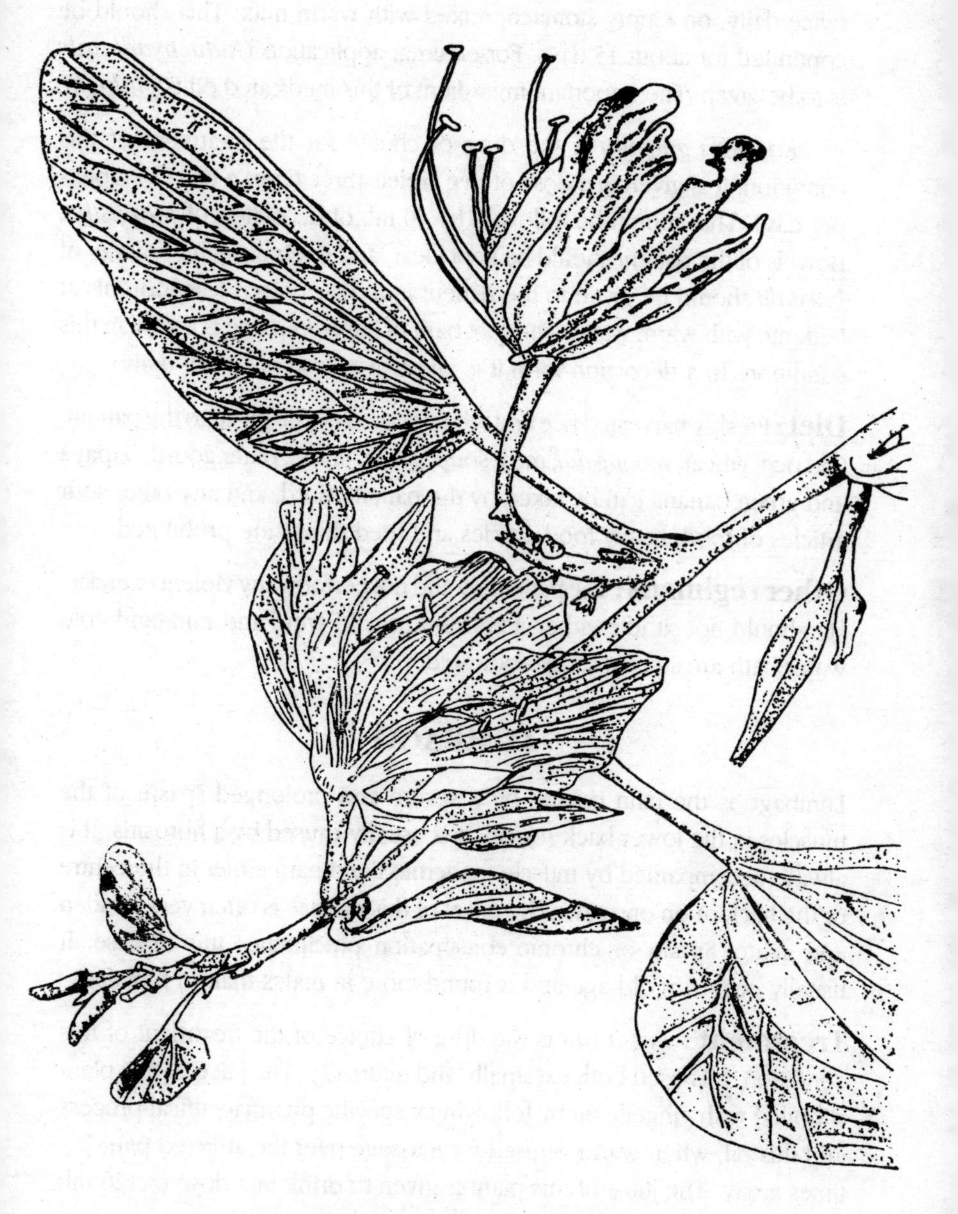

Fig. 20 *Bauhinia variegata* (*kanchanara*)

Treatment: Since this disease is caused by *vata,* in the beginning *Panchatikta ghrita* is given to the patient in a dose of two teaspoonfuls twice daily, on empty stomach, mixed with warm milk. This should be continued for about 15 days. For external application *Guduchyadi taila* is to be given. The important ingredient of this medicated oil is *guduchi.*

Kaishora guggulu is the drug of choice for the treatment of this condition. It is given in a dose of five tablets three times a day (15 tablets per day). This should be followed by 60 ml. of decoction of *manjistha.* Bowels of the patient should be kept clear, and if required the powder of *haritaki* should be given to the patient in a dose of two teaspoonfuls at bedtime with warm water. The root bark of *ashvattha* tree is useful in this condition. In a decoction form it is given in a dose of 60 ml. daily.

Diet : Freshly harvested rice and wheat should not be given to the patient. Old rice, wheat, *moong dal,* meat soup, garlic, onion, bitter gourd, papaya and green banana can be taken by the patient. Curd, and any other sour articles of food, heavy food articles and fried things are prohibited.

Other regimens : The patient should not perform any violent exercise. He should not sit idle either. Exposure to cold wind and rain, and cold water bath are strictly contra-indicated.

LUMBAGO

Lumbago is the pain caused by a severe and prolonged spasm of the muscles in the lower back region. It is usually caused by a fibrositis. It is always accompanied by muscle tenderness and pain either in the centre or the back or on one side. The onset of this disease is often very sudden and acute. Sprain or chronic constipation precipitates this disease. It usually occurs in old age and is found more in males than in females.

Treatment : *Prasarani* is the drug of choice of the treatment of this condition. It is used both externally and internally. The juice of this plant is boiled with gingelly oil by following a specific pharmaceutical process and this oil, when warm, is used for massage over the afflicted part, 2-3 times a day. The juice of this plant is given to drink in a dose of 120 ml. three times a day. The leaves of this plant produce a peculiar foetid-odour but when crushed with a pestle and mortar, the foetid odour disappears. To make it tasteful and more effective, a spoon of honey and 1/4th teaspoonful of black pepper powder are added to this dose. For relieving constipation, the patient should be regularly given castor oil in a suitable dose early in the morning. Ayurvedic physicians prefer raw castor oil which is given to the patient early morning in a dose of 1 teaspoonful mixed with a glass of milk. At times it produces very strong purgative action. To be on the safe side, the refined castor oil of B.P. or I.P. quality may by given to the patient in a dose which gives him clear motions. This should be repeated daily for about two months or till the pain is over. *Prasarani* should be taken for about a month. Even after the pain is subsided, there is every possibility that this may recur if proper care is not taken.

Diet: Sour and fried things and pulses are strictly prohibited in this condition. Wheat, *bajra* and *jawar* are better than rice.

Other regimens : After taking food, the patient should be advised to walk or lie down. He should not sit for 15 minutes. Sedentary habit is harmful for such patients. Some physical exercises which involve the movement of the muscles in the back and pelvic region are good for the patients. Morning walk is useful. Exposure to cold, strain and weight-lifting are strictly prohibited.

OBESITY

An excessive accumulation of fat in the body is called obesity. In Ayurveda this condition is called *medoroga*. There are many places in the body where excessive fat is accumulated. The most common areas are the abdomen, breasts and buttocks. The fat in the body is primarily drawn from the oils, ghees and other fatty substances consumed through food and drink. Normally this fat, during the process of metabolism, produces energy and heat. Fat also enters into the composition of some tissue cells in the human body. For example, the covering material over the nerve fibers contains a type of fatty material. The tissue cells of the brain and the muscles also contain fat. Nature has provided fat to accumulate in some of the joints to avoid friction during movement.

Fat in the body is also synthesised from the starchy material taken along with food. When fatty or starchy ingredients of food are taken in excess, fat in excess of the requirement of the body gets deposited in parts of the body. A by-product of fat called cholesterol circulates in the blood vessels and gets deposited in the walls of the vessel resulting in high blood pressure. Excessive fat may also impair the function of the vital organs like heart, liver and the kidneys. It may also result in diabetes. The most common difficulty the patient experiences because of excessive fat is breathlessness on even slight exertion. Such types of patients may even get afflicted by a serious type of asthma.

Intake of fats and carbohydrates in excess results in obesity. Lack of exercise also helps in the accumulation of fat in the body. Lack of mental work helps in the synthesis of fat from the carbohydrates taken through the food and instead of being consumed, gets deposited in the body.

Treatment : The patient should be asked to take up physical as well as mental exercise and should be asked to give up sedentary habits. Persons working in offices should have a little walk after taking their food. *Guggulu* is the drug of choice for the treatment of this condition. The gun-resin extracted from this plant is used in medicine. It is also used for the purpose of incense like *agarbatti* and *dhup. Guggulu* is purified by a special process before it is administered internally. For purification, this gum is boiled with the decoction of *triphala* and then strained though a cloth. This is given in a dose of one gm. four times a day followed by a cup of hot drink of choice. There are many compound preparations to which *guggulu* is added as the principal ingredient. The most important ones are *Navaka guggulu* and *triphala guggulu*. They are available in tablets of 0.125 gm each. Four tablets of this compound preparation are to be given to the patient four times a day (a total of 16 tablets a day) After the intake of this medicine, some hot drink should be given to the patient.

Diet: The patient should, as far as possible, avoid taking sweet and fatty things. Rice and potato which contain a lot of carbohydrates should be avoided. Among the cereals, wheat is better, and the patient can be given barley and maize also. Bitter and pungent things are good. Vegetables like bitter gourd, bitter variety of drumstick, *patola,* are useful for the patient. The patient can be given tea and coffee in good quantity. Intake of tabacco for persons who are not habituated with it, helps in the reduction of fat. This should be given to the patient only in small quantity as a medicine because it has many adverse effects on the body.

Haritaki is very useful in this condition. It helps in the clearance of the bowels and works as a tonic for the body. The pulp of this fruit should be crushed to a powder and given to the patient in a dose of one teaspoonful at bedtime with a cup of hot water. This should be given daily. In the beginning the patient may have loose motions. But after some time his body gets used to it and it no longer has purgative effect. *Murabba* prepared from this fruit can be given to the patient every day in place of the powder.

Other regimens: The patient should resort to physical and mental exercise and he should not sleep during daytime. Sleeping late at night and getting up early in the morning is very useful.

RHEUMATISM

Rheumatism is a disease marked by inflammation and pain in joints and muscles, usually recurrent and often caused due to exposure to cold. It is at times associated with fever. If not treated in time it may affect the heart. In Ayurveda this is known as *amavata*. This disease is caused by the production and circulation of a substance called *ama* in the body. This *ama* is produced by improper digestion as well as metabolism, and it gets lodged in joints etc., to produce inflammation and pain. Usually persons with constipative tendency and dietetic irregularity are affected by *amavata*.

Treatment : The choicest medicines for the treatment of this condition are and *Simhanada guggulu*. The chief ingredient of these and such other medicines for the treatment of this disease, is *guggulu*.

For patients having constipative tendency *Simhanada guggulu* is more useful. For other types of patients, *Mahayogaraja guggulu* is a better medicine. The dose of both of them is, in the beginning, two tablets three times a day. After the intake of this medicine, healthy patients should be given a cup of warm water. For weak and emaciated patients, a cup of milk is indicated.

The dose of this medicine should be slowly increased. In divided dose, about twenty tablets can be given to a patient per day. These medicines have no toxic effect whatsoever. But the patient may, at times, feel a little

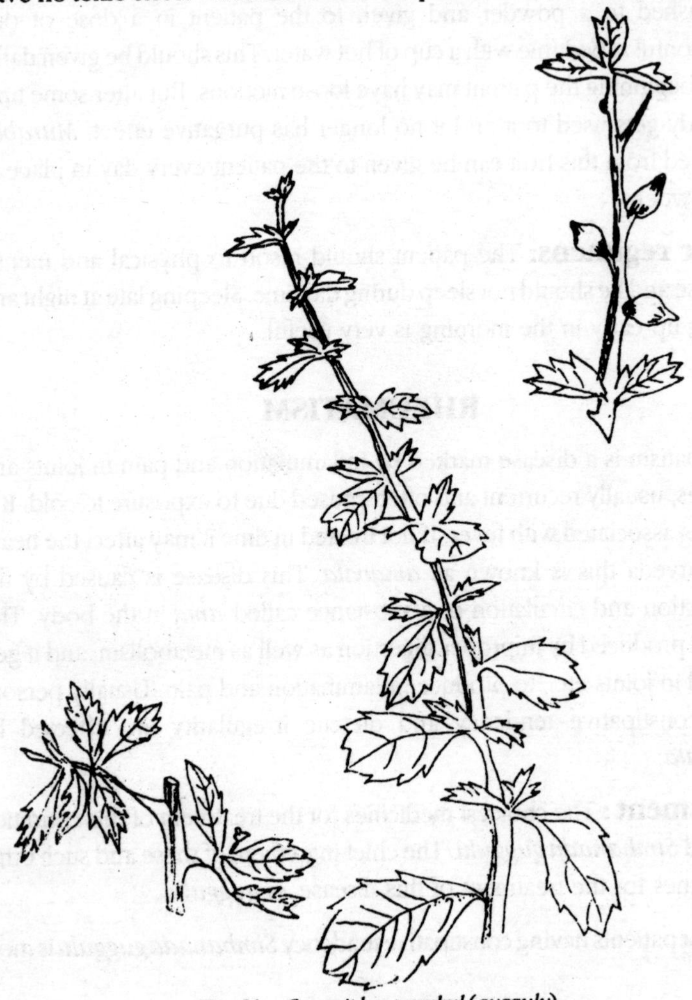

Fig. 21 *Commiphora mukul (guggulu)*

warmth in the body and in that case the dose should be reduced. In winter season these medicines are well tolerated.

These medicines show marked efficacy only when the patient who uses them is having clear motion. To remove constipation in a patient suffering from rheumatism, castor oil is considered to be the best purgative. Apart from the purgative effect, various parts of the plant, viz., seeds, roots leaves etc., are known to have anti-inflammatory effect when used both externally and internally. The next best medicine for the clearance of the bowel is the powder of *haritaki*.

A medicated oil known as *Saindhavadi taila* is recommended for external use. It should be applied over the affected joints and rubbed gently. It can be used for massage on other parts of the body as well.

Diet: Curd, other sour things, pulses and their preparations (except *moong dal*) are contra-indicated in this condition. Fried things and exceedingly cold things should be avoided as far as possible.

Other regimens: Sleep during daytime is prohibited. The patient should resort to only restricted physical exercise. Long walks at a fast speed and any exercise involving violent movement of the affected joints should be avoided.

RHEUMATOID ARTHRITIS

Rheumatoid arthritis is a generally progressive disease affecting primarily the joints which become swollen and painful. If not treated immediately, it may result in deformity. The muscles, ligaments, synovial membrane and the cartilages get inflamed and, therefore, movement of the joints becomes extremely painful. If it goes unchecked, and the joint remains immobilised for long periods, ankylosis occurs. This leads to deformity and difficulty in movement.

Treatment : In the beginning, *Mahayogaraj guggulu* is given to the patient. In winter season it is given in a dose of two tablets four times a days. In summer season it is given in a dose of two tablets, two times a day. Hot water or milk is given to the patient after these tablets. They are more effective when taken on empty stomach. Medicated oil, namely,

Mahanarayana taila should be used for gentle massage over the joints. In winter season, it should be slightly warmed before massage.

In the beginning, this disease affects the small joints in fingers. It is usually insidious. Stiffness of the small muscles of the hands is generally the next event and the fingers tend to get curved and ultimately become fixed. The infection then spreads towards the trunk involving the wrist joints, ankle joints, elbow joints, knee joints, shoulders, hips and jaw. If the bigger joints are affected then *Brihadvata chintamani* is the drug of choice. It is given in a dose of 0.250 gm., two or three times a day, depending upon the intensity of the pain and the duration of the disease. This is usually available in a powder form and given to the patient by mixing with honey.

At a later stage, even the spine gets affected and in that case, *Brihadvata chintamani* has to be given to the patient in a little higher dose for about a week and then reduced.

Both *Mahayogaraj guggulu* and *Brihadvata chintamani* will work in the body of the patient only if there is no constipation. The patient should, therefore, be given castor oil as purgative every evening. Apart from purgative effect, castor oil also exercises some therapeutic effect on the joints of the patient.

If the condition of the patient has become chronic, then along with *Mahayogaraj guggulu* or *Brihadvata chintamani*, a decoction called *Maharasanadi kwattha* should be given to the patient. It is given in a dose of 6 teaspoonfuls and it acts better if it is slightly warmed when administered.

Diet: Sour things, including curd, are strictly prohibited. Pulses and preparations of pulses, fried things and constipating foods should be shunned. Garlic and ginger are extremely useful for the patient. Five cloves of garlic should be given to the patient twice daily, along with food. If raw garlic is not tolerated for its foul odour, then it should be slightly fried in butter and given to the patient. Bitter vegetables like bitter gourd, bitter variety of drumstick and *neem* flowers are very good for the patient. Rice should be avoided.

Other regimens : Because of the inflammation, the patient is advised not to make much of movement, but he should not keep those joints immobilised. This may result in permanent deformity. Therefore light and gentle exercise are always needed for the patient. He should not expose himself to cold wind or rain. Taking bath in cold water is also to be avoided. He should not drink iced water. There should be sufficient gap between the intake of supper and going to bed. It is better if the food is taken at about 6 o'clock and the patient is allowed to go to bed by 9 or 9.30 p.m.

in this condition.

Other regimens : Sexual intercourse should be avoided and the patient should take plenty of liquid.

CHAPTER 13

DISEASES OF URINARY SYSTEM

BED-WETTING

It is involuntary urination at night. Children after the age of 3 or 4 years normally possess sufficient control over their urinary sphincters inasmuch as they pass urine only whenever they want. Because of certain reasons, this control does not manifest because of which they continue to pass urine in bed at night. This phenomenon continues in some cases, even up to the age of 15. Both the boys and girls suffer from this ailment, but boys outnumber girls in this respect.

Bed-wetters may pass urine at night even more than once. It is often found that the brothers and sisters of the patient used to pass urine involuntarily at night and it is also recorded that the parents in their young age had also the same trouble.

The causative factors of bed-wetting are two, namely, physical and emotional. If there is an infection in the bladder or kidney or an organic defect in the urinary tracts, the child may wet the bed. Sometimes, thread worms play a mischievous role. At night they come out of the anus to lay the eggs outside. While doings so, they cause a certain amount of irritation and as a reflex action the child passes urine. Other intestinal worms are also found to cause this problem. They cause some amount of pain in the stomach and as a reflex action, the child passes urine.

The psychic factors are (i) too early an attempt for bladder training, (ii) emotional immaturity, (iii) shyness, (iv) conflicts between parents, (v) conflict between the child and his parents, (vi) rivalry among brothers and sisters, (vii) insufficient attention from the parents, (viii) sense of insecurity, and (ix) problems of school adjustment. Sometimes the children get nightmares and they are mostly thumb suckers or nail biters.

Treatment: The cause of the disease should first be located and if it is physical or emotional it should be correctly treated. The child should not be scolded and after 4 o'clock, he should not be given any water to drink even if he feels thirsty. He should have dinner without water or much of fluid. The parents should find out approximately the time of bed-wetting and should wake up the child about 1/2 hour before that and take him to the bathroom. As a practice the child should be asked to urinate before going to bed. When he is awakened from his sleep, he should not be carried to the bathroom by his parents when he is half asleep. He should be made to get up from his bed and visit the bathroom himself for passing the urine. A system of rewards for dry nights often serves as an added incentive and often helps in stopping the bad habit.

In Ayurveda, the child is given medicines to strengthen his nervous system and the urinary tract. Unless there is an organic defect in the urinary tract, these medicines, if used continuously for sufficiently long time, help the child to get control over his urinary sphincters and thus he stops bed-wetting. The medicine that is commonly used for this purpose is *shilajit*. To a child of five years, this medicine can be given in a dose of 1/4th of a gram twice daily, mixed with milk on empty stomach. For young boys and girls of the age of 15 it can be given in a dose of 1/2 gm. twice daily. It produces a sense of warmth in the body of the patient when taken continuously for a long time. It is, therefore, well-tolerated during winter season and in summer, its dose should be reduced to 50%.

There are many medicines containing *shilajit* as an important ingredient. The one popularly used for bed-wetting by ayurvedic physicians is *Chandra probha vati*. Normally tablets of this medicine are available and they weigh 0.250 gm. To children of about five years age, half a tablet of this medicine is given in the morning and another half in the evening on empty stomach with half a cup of milk. Children of more than 10 years of age can take one full tablet, twice daily with milk. This medicine is specific for geneto-urinary complaints. It strengthens the geneto-urinary tract and simultaneously strengthens the nervous system.

Diet: As has already been suggested before, the patient should stop taking water after 4 o'clock in the afternoon and no liquids should be given to him during night meals. Food ingredients which are spicy, which cause constipation and wind formation in the stomach, particularly pulses, are strictly prohibited. The patient should take patola, bitter gourd, pumpkin, gourd, potato, tomato, cauliflower, cabbage, spinach, radish, drumsticks and other leafy vegetables.

Other regimens : The patient's bowels should be kept clear so that thread worms do not trouble him at night. This is one of the important causes of bed-wetting. He should be shown affection, and an atmosphere of friendship should be created amongst his brothers and sisters. He should not be made to sleep on rubber bed mattresses. This causes disturbances in his sleep and he is likely to pass urine at night. Parents should take the child for a walk every evening. This helps the child to overcome the defect, both physically and emotionally. He feels secure and thus overcomes the fear complex which is one of the important emotional agents for bed-wetting.

BURNING URINE

While passing urine, some people feel burning sensation in the urinary passage. An infection in the urinary passage caused by venereal diseases like gonorrhoea, enlargement of prostrate, a stone in the urinary bladder, or simple concentrated urine, as it happens in summer, might be responsible for this type of complaint. The burning sensation may occur along with the passage of urine or it may occur even after that. It may subside by taking some alkaline drinks or few glasses of simple water. It may occur during daytime or night-time. Other symptoms like discharge of pus from the urethra, stoppage of urination, bleeding and fever might accompany.

Treatment : The main disease because of which burning sensation occurs in the urinary passage has to be treated meticulously. There are some ayurvedic medicines which specially act to correct the burning sensation. They are *gokshura, chandan, ushira* and *shilajatu.* Many preparations of these medicines are also available and they are commonly administered to such patients. *Gokshuradi guggulu* and *Chandra probha vati* are given to the patients in a dose of two tablets, three or four times a day, depending upon the seriousness of the disease. They not only reduce the burning sensation but also act as an antiseptic while being eliminated through the urinary tract. They are used both for preventive and curative purposes. *Chandanasava* and *Ushirasava* are two alcoholic preparations. They are given to the patient in a dose of six teaspoonfuls after food, twice daily with equal quantity of water. They also have antiseptic effect on the geneto-urinary tract.

Among animal products, *pravala* is considered to be extremely useful for the treatment of burning sensation in any part of the body. If the complaint is chronic, the patient has to be given *pravala* in a powder form. It is made to a powder by grinding with rose water. This is usually given in a dose of 0.5 gm. twice daily, mixed with milk.

Diet: Hot spices are to be strictly avoided. The patient should be given as much water as possible to drink. Fresh lemon juice, fresh coconut water, orange juice, sugarcane juice, and pineapple juice are extremely useful in this condition. The patient should be given fruits like apple, grapes, peaches and plums in good quantity. The juice of radish and its leaves should be given to the patient in a dose of 30 ml. twice daily. Carrot juice is also very useful in the condition.

Rice, ghee, milk and leafy vegetables are also very useful for the patient.

Other regimens: The patient should not expose himself to sun or heat. Excessive perspiration takes away lot of water from the body and the urine thus becomes concentrated. Passage of this concentrated urine through the urinary tract causes irritation and gives rise to burning sensation.

In summer season, burning urine commonly occurs along with heat stroke. Before going out in the sun, it is always advisable to take a glass

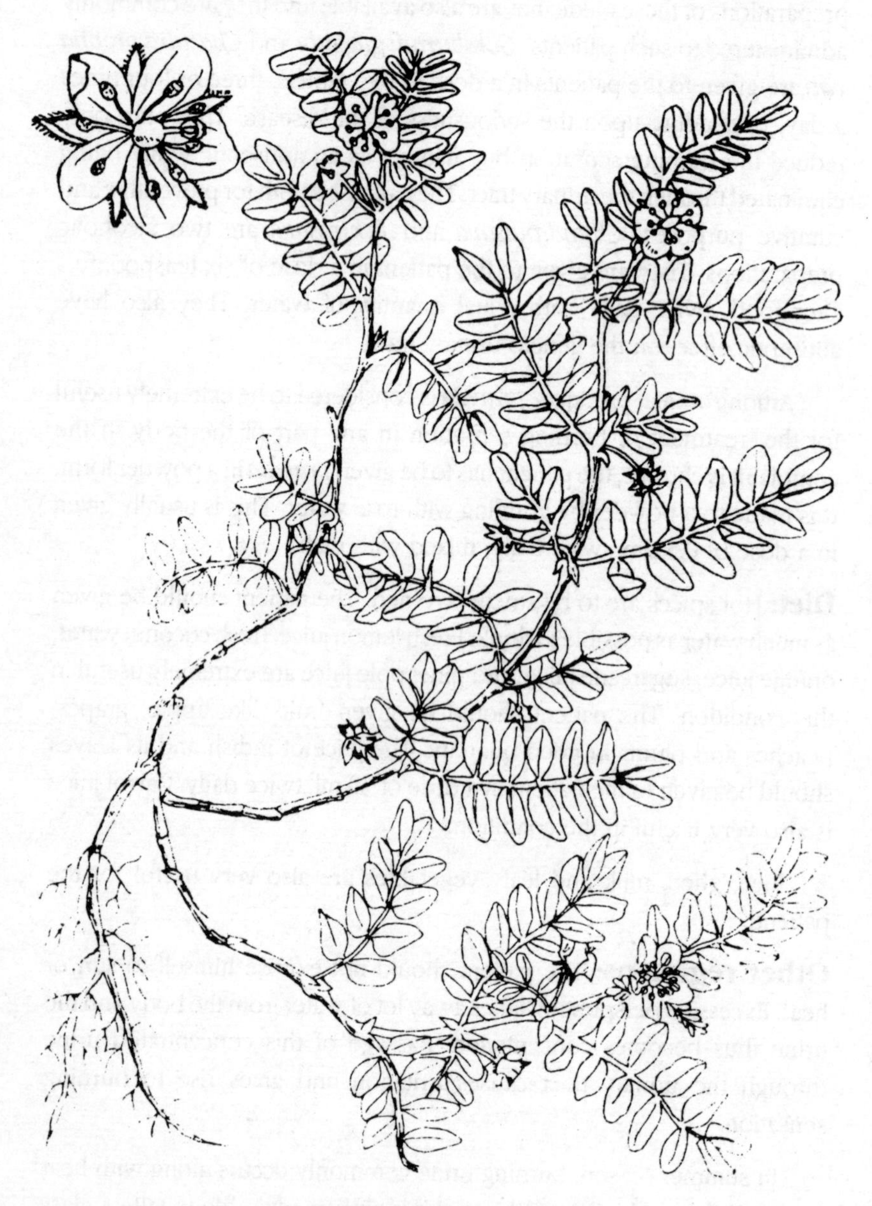

Fig. 22 *Tributus terrestris (gokshura)*

or two of syrup prepared by boiling green mango and adding sugar to it. *Jamun* is a very useful fruit for this complaint. Two or three glasses of water mixed with *gur* should be taken early morning every day, during summer season.

NEPHRITIS

Ordinarily this means inflammation of the kidney. It is of several types and in different stages of the disease it produces different types of symptoms. In Ayurveda it is called *vrikka shotha.*

Depending upon the variety of the nephritis, the signs and symptoms considerably vary. Usually there is oedema in the face, which is more prominent in the morning and slowly subsides as the day passes on. The urine may contain albumen or even blood. The blood pressure may increase and the patient may suffer from biliouness, nausea, vomiting, abdominal pain, headache and diarrhoea. He usually passes less quantity of urine and if not attended to in time, this may lead to many serious complications.

Treatment : *Punarnava mandoora* is the drug of choice for the treatment of this condition. It is available in a powder form and given to the patient in a dose of 1 gm. three times per day mixed with honey. If there is chronic fever associated with nephritis, then the patient should be given *Suvarna vasanta malati.* It is given in a dose of 0.250 gm. twice a day, mixed with honey. This medicine contains gold in *bhasma* form which acts as an antibiotic in the body and subsides inflammation.

Diet : The patient should be given less of salt and lot of water. Fried things, sour things, specially curd, are strictly prohibited. If there is less of urine, the patient should be given the juice of radish in a dose of 300 ml. two or three times a day.

Other regimens : The patient should be given complete rest and not be permitted to remain awake late at night. If it is associated with fever, cough and cold, the patient should not be permitted to go out-doors. In chronic nephritis the patient should move about, because walking helps him considerably. If there is constipation, steps should be taken to correct it immediately, *Triphala* powder in a dose of one teaspoonful is very helpful to relieve the constipation of such patients. This can be given to the patient every day at bedtime with a cup of milk or hot water.

PROSTATE ENLARGEMENT

The prostate gland is a part of the male genital apparatus, located near and surrounding the outlet of the urinary bladder. Its main function is to secrete a liquid which forms a part of seminal fluid. A condition in which this gland slowly gets enlarged over a period of years, is known as the benign enlargement of the prostate. In this condition, usually the entire gland is enlarged. If there is infection or cancer, then even a portion of the gland may get enlarged.

Since it is part of the male genital apparatus, this gland normally gets enlarged in almost all males in the age between 40 and 45; but most men go about with this slightly enlarged prostate, without experiencing difficulty. It is a manifestation of the normal process of ageing.

When the gland is abnormally enlarged, it interferes with normal urination. The enlarged gland compresses the outlet of the bladder and this may result in a sudden inability to urinate. The common symptoms of the enlargement of prostate are increase in frequency of urination during daytime and the patient has to pass urine many times at night. He develops a sense of hesitation in starting the flow of urine and the stream of urine gets diminished in size and force. There is a burning sensation during urination. At times there is complete suppression of urination with blood coming out with the urine.

Treatment : *Shilajit* is considered to be the best medicine for the treatment of benign enlargement of prostate gland.

It is used in a dose of 1/2 teaspoonful at bedtime with milk. It generates heat inside the body. Therefore, it is very well tolerated during winter season and in cold countries where it can be administered even two or three times a day. But, in hot countries, and in summer season it has to be used only in a small dose. However, taking this medicine with milk reduces its heating effect on the body considerably and it increase its rejuvenating and aphrodisiac effects.

There are many preparations of *shilajit*. The most commonly used one is *Chandra prabha vati*. It is available in a tablet form and used in a dose of two tablets, three times a day with milk. This medicine has to be used for a considerably longer time. One has to take it even for years together. Even after the symptoms of prostate enlargement have subsided, the medicine has to be used for about six months more with a view to prevent the recurrence of prostate enlargement.

Diet: Sour things and fried things are harmful for the patient. Cow's ghee, butter, milk, garlic, ginger and asafoetida are very useful for this condition.

Other regimens: Excessive sexual intercourse is one of the important reasons for the abnormal enlargement of the prostate gland. After the prostate enlargement has taken place, sexual intercourse should be avoided. Suppression of the urge for urination is not desirable. Therefore, whenever there is a feeling for urination, the patient should be advised to attend to it immediately. Constipation is one of the important precipitating factors for this disease. The bowels of the patient should be kept clean either through a laxative or by taking such food ingredients which help in bowel movement. Sedentary habit is very bad for patients having enlarged prostate. Sitting on a chair immediately after taking food is not advisable — one should lie down for about 15 minutes after taking food. Both for prevention and cure of this disease, walking for about 3 kilometers a day would be very useful.

STONES IN THE URINARY TRACT

Urinary stones are generally formed by calcium, phosphates or oxalates. The main parts of the urinary tract are the kidney, ureter, bladder and urethra. The stones are formed primarily in the kidney and sometimes remain there without being noticed for a long time. In certain circumstances they are slowly dissolved or dislodged and come down, and during this process, they become lodged in a narrow part of the tract giving rise to excruciating pain.

Stones are formed in the body because of *vayu*. It creates a type of dryness in the body because of which the chemicals start accumulating over a nucleus, that ultimately takes the shape of a stone. At times the entire kidney is filled with these stones, becomes calcified and stops functioning. If urine is not excreted through the kidneys or excreted in small quantities, uremia sets in and causes many complications. The same phenomenon takes place if a piece of stone gets lodged in ureter or bladder.

The patient experiences pain in the lumber region of the kidneys at the back of the body. The pain radiates towards the genital organs. There might be fever, vomiting, loss of appetite, sleeplessness and painful urination. At times blood may appear in the urine.

Treatment: *Pashanabheda* is the drug of choice for the treatment of this disease. The rhizome of this plant is used in medicine. It is given in the form of a powder in the dose of one teaspoonful three times a day. It can be given in the form of a decoction also in a dose of 30 ml. three times a day.

Varuna is the other drug which is popularly used for this condition. The bark of this tree is boiled with water and the decoction thus prepared is given to the patient in a dose of 30 ml. three times a day.

Gokshuradi guggulu is very useful when, due to the stone there is obstruction to the passage of urine. *Gokshura* is known for its diuretic property and guggulu helps in the alleviation of *vayu*. This compound preparation, therefore, helps both in the cure and prevention of this disease.

The most important drug used in this condition is *shilajit* (rock exudation-bitumen). Because of its therapeutic efficacy in diseases of the urino-genital tract and its short supply, it is a little difficult to obtain *shilajit* of good quality. Now-a-days this drug is being commonly manufactured by boiling stones having *shilajatu* in them. The dose of this drug is one teaspoonful twice daily and it is given with warm milk. *Chandra prabha vati* and *shilajatvadi lauha* are two of the important preparations of this drug.

Diet: The patient should not take beans and pulses. Yellow variety of pumpkin, colocasia and lady's fingers are strictly prohibited. White variety of pumpkin and gourd are very useful in this condition.

Other regimens : The patient should not sit continuously for a long time. Immediately after taking food he should either walk for a few minutes or lie down. Sitting in the office constantly for a long time is also prohibited. He should sit on a soft cushion and move about for a few minutes after working for about one hour. He should not remain constipated, because constipation aggravates *vayu* which helps in the formation of stones. A laxative should, therefore, be taken almost everyday. The patient should develop the habit of drinking plenty of water which will help him micturate frequently. This will cleanse the urinary system and will prevent the formation of stones. Occasionally stones which are already formed will break into pieces as they are dissolved and are passed out in the form of gravel or sand.

HEMATURIA

Presence of blood in the urine is called hematuria. According to Ayurveda it is a form of *adhoga rakta pitta*. It is commonly caused by stones or infection in the genito-urinary tract and some other haemorrhagic conditions. The patient may pass urine mixed with blood and at times he will micturate blood alone.

Treatment : *Gokshura* is the drug of choice for this condition. The seed of this plant is used in the medicine. It is given in the form of a powder in a dose of one teaspoonful twice a day, mixed with honey. It is also given in the form of a decoction in a dose of 50 ml., two times a day. *Guduchi* is popularly used for the treatment of this condition. The juice of this plant is given to the patient in a dose of 30 ml. three times a day. Both the stem and the leaves are used for the extraction of the juice. The starch collected from the matured stem of this plant is called *Guduchi sattva*. This is given to the patient in a dose of one teaspoonful three times a day with milk or water.

Shilajit is very effective in curing hematuria. It is given to the patient in a dose of one teaspoonful twice daily along with milk. In the winter season this drug is tolerated very well.

Diet: Vegetable prepared from green banana, *patola,* bitter gourd and drumstick are very useful in this condition. Old rice, wheat, meat soup and *moong dal* can be given to the patient. Hot and spicy food should be avoided. White pumpkin should be given to the patient in large quantity. One or two glasses of juice of white pumpkin mixed with sugarcane juice can be given every day. Pomegranate and *amalaki* in any form are useful in this condition.

Other regimens : Sexual intercourse should be avoided and the patient should take plenty of liquid.

CHAPTER 14

DISEASES OF EAR, NOSE AND THROAT

EPISTAXIS

Bleeding from the nose is called epistaxis. According to Ayurveda, it is a form of *urdhvaga rakta pitta.* It is usually associated with nasal polyp. During summer, this occurs often, specially in small children. Exposure to sun or fire, high blood pressure and infection in the nose precipitate the attack.

Treatment : The patient having epistaxis should be given a wash of his face and head with cold water. Cold water can be given for inhalation as well. He should not sneeze or put any type of strain on the nose which aggravates bleeding.

Durva is the ideal drug for this condition. The juice of this grass is to be poured into the nose, about ten drops in each nostril, and deeply inhaled. Similarly, the juice of the flower of pomegranate should be given to the patient for deep inhalation. If the patient suffers from repeated attacks of epistaxis, then during the period when there is no attack, he should be given *Anu taila* for inhalation, in a dose of ten drops in each nostril.

Vasavaleha may be given to the patient in a dose of one teaspoonful three times a day with honey or milk. Nasal polyp usually occurs in patients suffering from chronic cold and chronic constipation. In such cases *Chyavana prasha* can be given to the patient in a dose of one teaspoonful two times a day with milk.

Diet : The patient should not be given any hot or spicy things to eat. Grapes, white pumpkin, meat soup, soup of *moong dal,* old rice, pomegranate, butter and cow's milk can be given to the patient.

Fig. 23 *Cynodon dactylon* (*durva*)

Other regimens : The patent should not expose himself to hard physical or mental labour. He should have his blood pressure checked. If the blood pressure is high, hasty steps should not be taken to check the bleeding from the nose, because it works as a safety valve. The patient should not be permitted to remain awake late in the night.

GLOSSITIS

Inflammation of mucous membrane over the tongue is known as glossitis. In Ayurveda this is called *jibvapaka.* It is usually caused by the intake of alcohol, spices, smoking, gastrointestinal as well as metabolic diseases.

The tongue becomes red and at times there are ulcers also. The patient feels difficulty in taking his food.

Treatment : Alum is very popularly used for the treatment of this disease. In Ayurveda this is called *sphatika*. It is fried in a frying pan and gets dehydrated and swollen and the colour changes to white. Then it is powdered and the powder is also added to a cup of warm water in a dose of 1/2 teaspoonful and this warm water is used for gargling 2 to 3 times a day.

Diet : Glossitis does not permit the patient to chew his food. It is, therefore, advisable to give thin gruel prepared of rice, barley or arrowroot. Turmeric powder is very useful in healing the ulcers. This is normally used in condiments. To a cup of milk, about 1/2 teaspoonful of turmeric powder should be added and mixed well. If required, a spoon of sugar can be added to it to make it tasteful. This is to be given to the patient two times a day. This reduces the inflammation and helps in removing constipation.

Other regimens : Taking a glass of cold water early in the morning after getting up from the bed, helps in the prevention as well as cure of glossitis.

HOARSENESS OF VOICE

The inflammation of the throat including pharynx and larynx causes hoarseness of voice. In Ayurveda this is called *svarabheda*.

Infection, intake of exceedingly hot and cold drinks, an abnormal growth, foreign material, infection of lungs by tuberculosis are some of the main factors responsible for the causation of this ailment.

The patient may not be able to speak easily or there might be pain during speech. It might be associated with fever and cough. The tongue remains usually coated, and the conditions aggravated when the patient is constipated.

Treatment : The patient should be given the powder of *yashtimadhu* and *vacha* in a dose of one teaspoonful, four times a day mixed with honey. Dry hot fomentation externally is very useful in this condition. Gargle by adding a teaspoonful of *Irimedadi taila* in a cup of lukewarm water is very useful in this condition. *Khadiradi vati* or *Eladi vati* should be kept in mouth and chewed slowly. If there is constipation, the patient should be given the powder of *haritaki* in a dose of one teaspoonful at bedtime with hot water.

Diet : Ginger, black pepper, salt, garlic, dry grapes and ghee are useful in this condition. The patient should avoid curd, other sour things, fried things and exceedingly cold things.

Other regimens : The patient should not expose his throat to cold wind or cold water. He should avoid taking head bath for a few days.

PUS IN THE EAR

In Ayurveda this condition is known as *putikarna*. Inflammation of the ear is caused by some organisms. These organisms flourish when the patient is suffering from cold, cough and sinusitis. Small children are commonly affected by this ailment. At times, feeding milk to the child forcibly results in the milk coming to the middle and the external ears. This leads to inflammation and pus formation.

When pus comes from the ear, it produces a foul smell. There is acute pain and the child cries. It is usually associated with cough and even at times with fever. *Kapha dosha* is primarily responsible for all these manifestations.

Treatment : *Lakshmi vilasa rasa* is the drug of choice for the treatment of this condition. It is given internally to an adult in a dose of one pill three times a day, mixed with honey. To the children also it is given internally but in a reduced dose.

Nirgundi is the drug of choice for external use in the condition. The juice of the leave of this plant is mixed with mustard oil and boiled. This medicated oil is dropped into the ear twice daily.

In the similar way *bilva* is used in this condition. A paste of the root of the plant is boiled with mustard oil and after filtering, this medicated oil is used as ear drops.

Diet : Ingredients of food which aggravate *kapha* are prohibited. Curd, banana, guava and sour fruits should not be given to the patient. Intake of garlic, onion and ginger is very useful in this condition.

Other regimens : The patient should not take bath, nor should he expose himself to cold wind and rain.

PYORRHOEA

Pyorrhoea is characterised by copious discharge of pus from the root of the teeth and gums. Depending upon the part of the teeth and the gums involved, it is of several types. In Ayurveda, this condition is called *danta-veshta or putidanta*. The pus which comes out from the gums is often swallowed along with the food articles and this produces many types of diseases in the body, when it gets absorbed by the gastro-intestinal tract. It becomes difficult for the patient to chew and eat hard ingredients of food, because while chewing, there is pain and bleeding from the gums. This produces foul smell in the mouth, and teeth fall out one after the other because they become loose. Thus, it causes premature old-age and many other diseases in the body.

Infection by various types of germs is considered in allopathic system of medicine to be the cause of this condition. Non-observance of oral hygiene like brushing teeth daily, and cleaning the mouth after the intake of food is also responsible for this disease. In Ayurveda, all the causative factors are accepted. In addition, great emphasis is laid upon the digestion and movement of bowels. The mouth and its different parts, are considered to be the indicators of conditions prevailing in the gastro-intestinal tract including the liver and colon. A person having bad digestion and constipation is more prone to get pyorrhoea.

Treatment : The patient is invariably asked to adopt measures for oral hygiene like cleaning teeth with a soft brush and a suitable tooth powder or a tooth paste. Instead of using a nylon tooth brush, patients are usually advised to use the prop-root of banyan tree for brushing teeth. About 10 cm. of this root of the diameter of an ordinary pencil is selected for this purpose. Fresh prop-root gives better results. The latex or the milk which comes out of this prop-root is very helpful in preventing the formation of pus because of its antiseptic properties, and it stops bleeding because of its astringent properties. This prop root is required to be chewed for about 2 minutes to give a fine brush with which the teeth are to be cleaned. This chewing also helps in squeezing out the pus which is already accumulated at the root of the teeth. Twigs or tender branches of other trees like *neem* can also be used for the same purpose in the same manner.

To remove constipation the patient is given a decoction of *triphala*. *Triphala* consists of the fruits *amalaki, bibhitaki* and *hartaki*. Powders of the pulp of these fruits are taken in equal quantity and mixed well. Three grams of this powder should be added to 250 ml. of water and boiled till reduced to half. The powder should be strained and thrown away. Only the liquid portion when it is slightly warm is to be taken at bedtime. This gives a clear motion in the morning. The dose of this powder is to be adjusted depending upon the purgative action it produces on the body of the individual. This is to be taken daily at bedtime.

Powder of the bark of *bakula* and *babula* are very good for this condition. They are to be used as tooth powders for cleaning teeth once in the morning and once while going to bed.

The compound ayurvedic preparation which is very popularly used for this condition is known as *Dashana samskara churna*. This, when used either by finger or with the help of a soft brush for cleaning teeth, removes the foul smell of the mouth quickly and in about 15 days' time the pus formation and bleeding subside. The use of this powder for cleaning teeth is to be continued for about 3 months thereafter. Some people use it for cleaning teeth as a routine.

Diet : Food items which stick to the root of the teeth while eating should be avoided as far as possible. Ingredients of food which are sour in taste like pickles, curd and sour fruits are contra-indicated in this condition. Fruits which are not sour like apple, papaya and cucumber are considered useful. Fruits of guava, pomegranate and *amalaki* which contain a lot of vitamin C are very good in this condition. They are not harmful even though they are sour in taste. Vegetables, having bitter taste like *karela*, *patola* and drumstick are useful in this condition.

SNEEZING

Sneezing is a sudden and involuntary violent expiration preceded by inspiration. During sneezing, the mouth generally remains closed, so that the current of air is directed through the nose. The person sneezes normally because of some irritation in the mucous membrane of the nose, or the sinuses in the head. The phlegm that remains accumulated inside the sinus, gets cleared by this act of sneezing. Normally, the sneezing takes place once or twice in a day. When there is snow and cold, one sneezes much more. Often the attack of sneezing is repetitive to cause concern. Water comes out from nose and mouth. Sometimes when the patient gets up from the bed, he finds his nose completely blocked, and goes on sneezing. Taking of certain types of food like curd, banana, iced water, ice-cream precipitates these attacks of sneezing. Allergy is often considered to be one of the reasons for sneezing.

Treatment : *Haridra khanda* is the drug of choice for the treatment of this condition. It is prepared with turmeric and some other vegetable drugs. One teaspoonful of this powder is to be given to the patient 4 times a day, mixed with a cup of hot milk of warm water.

The patient should be given *Shadabindu taila,* or *Anu taila* for deep inhalation. The former is to be used in a dose of 6 drops in each nostril and the latter is to be used in a dose of 20 drops in each nostril. These medicated oils are to be deeply inhaled. These may provoke some more bouts of sneezing and running of water from the nose. This may happen for the first two days; thereafter the patient will not feel any discomfort and eventually use these nasal drops. For an adult, use of these nasal drops for about a month will be sufficient to relieve him of sneezing bouts.

The patients normally remain constipated. To keep their bowels clean *Agastya rasayana* should be given to them in a dose of 2-4 teaspoonfuls at bedtime with a cup of milk or warm water. Apart from relieving constipation, this medicine has a tonic effect on the body and specially on lungs, throat and the mucous membrane of the nose. This medicine should be given to the patient even after the sneezing bouts stop with a view to prevent recurrence of these attacks. Normally a six months' course of this medicine would be sufficient for an average patient.

Diet : Curd, banana, fried things and drinks added with ice are to be strictly prohibited. Eating of rice is not good for these patients. Turmeric, garlic, ginger and black pepper should be used in good quantities by these patients and they are always helpful both for the prevention as well as the cure of this disease. Apart from garlic that is added to the vegetables, the patient is advised to take about 10 cloves twice daily. This can be taken in raw form, but because of its strong smell, some people do not like it very much. In that case, it should be fried with butter or ghee; it becomes brown and odourless and then it should be given to the patient. This frying, while making it odourless, reduces the therapeutic efficacy of garlic. The patient should take a lot of leafy vegetables so that the bowels remain clean.

Other regimens : The patient should avoid taking head bath when having acute attacks of sneezing. Exposure to rain, or excessive cold wind, is very bad for the patient. Dust, and the smoke of factories are bad for the patient and should be avoided.

STOMATITIS

Inflammation of the mouth resulting in defuse redness, erosion, blisters and submucousal haemorrhages and ulcers is known as stomatitis. The tongue may also be affected simultaneously. In Ayurveda this is called *mukhapaka*.

It might be caused by different types of germs. It might also be a symptom of the toxity of the drugs and heavy metals. Nutritional deficiency may also be responsible for the causation of this disease. This may appear as a symptom of some other diseases also.

Treatment : The patient of this type normally remains constipated. He should be given a laxative and this should be repeated till the patient is cured. *Triphala* is the proper laxative for this purpose. *Haritaki, bibhitaki* and *amalaki* taken together are called *triphala.* The pulp of the fruit of these three is taken in equal quantity and kept in a powder form for use. This powder can be given daily to the patient in a dose of one teaspoonful at bedtime. The taste of this drug is astringent and, therefore, it may not be liked by the patient. It should, therefore, be mixed with a cup of milk to which half a teaspoonful of sugar should be added and mixed well and given to the patient at bedtime. If the bowels of the patient do not react to this properly, then the dose can be increased. This can be given to the patient in the form of decoction also. To a cup of water, one teaspoonful of this powder is to be added and boiled till half. Then it is to be filtered and given to the patient at bedtime. Because of its astringent taste, a teaspoonful of honey may be added to it and mixed well before it is administered to the patient.

Khadiradi vati is the drug of choice for the treatment of this condition. The main ingredient of this medicine is *khadira.* This medicine is available in tablet form. The patient should be given one tablet of this medicine to keep it in the mouth and slowly suck it as it dissolves in saliva. Like this, 6 to 8 tablets should be given to the patient per day. This prevents excessive saliva and produces a soothing effect on the ulcers and inflamed parts.

Irimedadi taila is also commonly used for the treatment of the condition. One teaspoonful of this medicated oil is added to a cup of warm water and the patient is given this mixture for gargling. This should be repeated 3-4 times a day.

Diet : The patient should take non-constipative diet, free from sour things, including curd and pickles and spices. Green vegetables and fruits should be given to the patient in considerable amount. Papaya and *surana* are very useful for the patient.

Other regimens : Those who suffer from Chronic stomatities should avoid using tobacco in any form. Use of tooth paste or tooth powder having *neem* in any form is extremely useful.

TONSILLITIS

Tonsils are the small rounded mass of mainly lymphoid tissue behind the

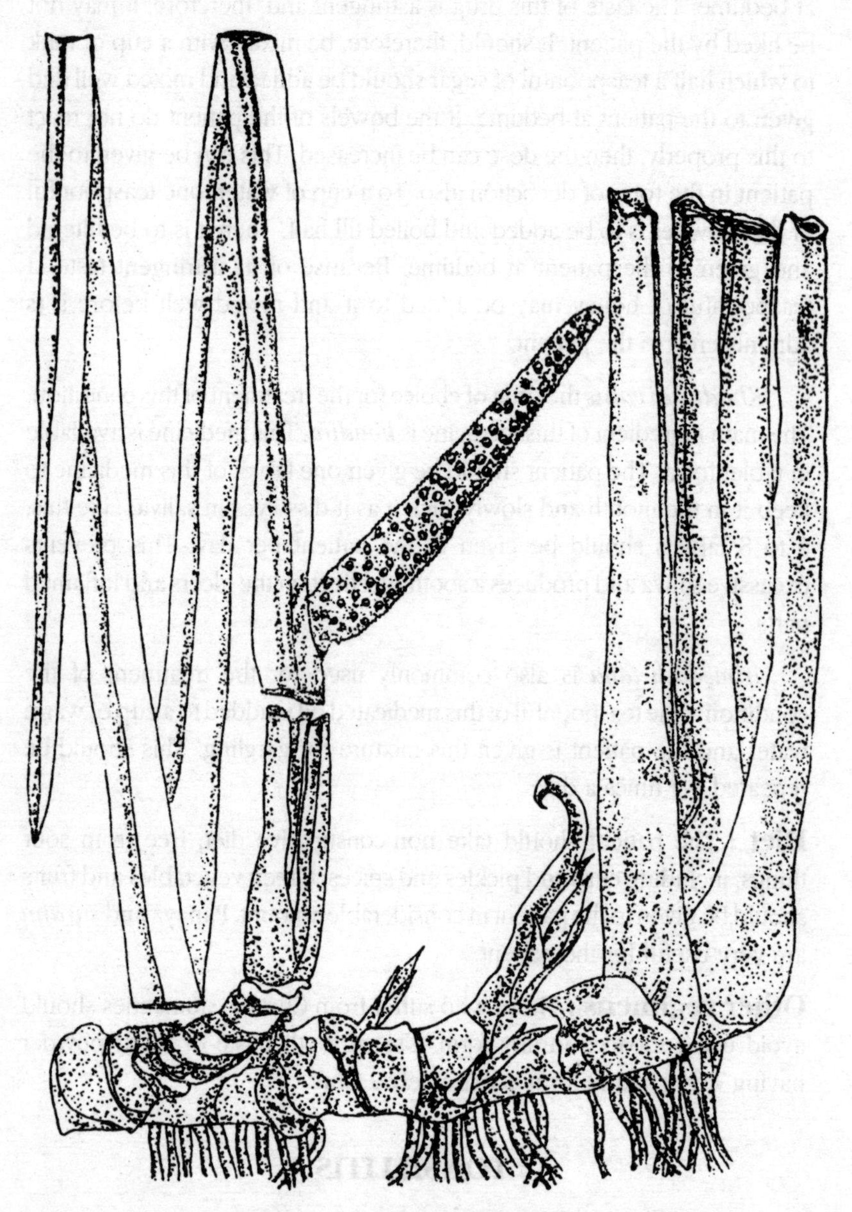

Fig. 24 *Acorus calamus* (*vacha*)

tongue between the pillars or the faucis on either side of the pharynx. Its inflammation is called tonsillitis. In Ayurveda it is known as *tundikeri*. It usually occurs in young children. It is often associated with attacks of cold and cough. Constipation precipitates the attack of this ailment.

The tonsils in the throat become red and swollen. The patient suffers from cough and pain in the throat. He experiences difficulty in swallowing food. Even breathing at times becomes difficult. In children it is often associated with fever. The tongue remains coated.

Treatment : The patient should be given hot fomentation externally on the front side of the neck and efforts should be made to keep it warm as long as possible. The bark of *babula* tree is very useful in this condition. The decoction of this bark mixed with rock-salt may be used as a gargle. The powder of *yashti madhu, vacha* and *kulanjana* are also used in the treatment of this condition. These three powders are made to a paste with honey and licked by the patient. This soothes the throat and cures inflammation.

Khadiradi vati is the drug of choice for the treatment of this condition. It is kept in the mouth and slowly sucked as it gets mixed up with the saliva of mouth. In this way five to six tablets can be taken per day.

Persons suffering from chronic tonsillitis should be given *Agastya rasayana* to be taken in a dose of one teaspoonful, twice daily mixed with honey. It should be given to the patient for about six months. Even if there is no tonsillitis, the patient should continue to take the medicine which produces immunity against the future attack of tonsillitis.

Diet : The patient can be given the soup of meat and pulses like *moong* and *kulattha*. He should be given *methi*, bitter gourd, *patola* and young radish. He should avoid dry, hard and heavy food, all sour things, curd, milk and sugarcane juice.

Other regimens : Sleep during day time and bath are prohibited. Care should be taken to keep the bowels of the patient clear.

(xxviii) *Kutajadi churna* : The woman who drinks in

CHAPTER 15

DISEASES OF HEAD

HEADACHE

THE TREATMENT of headache is a headache for physicians. This popular statement does not hold good for the practitioners of Ayurveda. In Ayurveda it is known as *shirahshula*. It is of several types depending upon the predominance of one or the other of the *doshas* in the pathogenesis of this disease.

Both physical and psychic factors are considered to be responsible for this disease. Defective eye-sight, inflammation of the sinus, high blood pressure, sleeplessness, tumour in the brain, prolonged over-work, emotional strain, exposure of the head to excessive heat, cold or sun-rays, indigestion, constipation and wind formation in the stomach among others, may produce headache. Headache is a symptom of many other diseases like fever, influenza and bronchitis.

Depending upon the domination of *doshas*, the signs and symptoms associated with headache vary. For example, in *shlaishmika* type of headache, there is always heaviness of the head, watering of the eyes, inflammation of the middle ear, running of the nose, inflammation of the mucous membrane of the nose, nasal polyp and many other similar symptoms. This type of headache generally occurs in the early morning, in rainy or winter season, and immediately after food. Children are more affected by this type of headache. *Paittika* type of headache is always associated with burning sensation in various parts of the head and bleeding from the nose. It generally aggravates during mid-day and summer and autumn seasons. The *vatika* type of headache is always associated with giddiness, dryness and roughness of the eyes and various type of pain in different organs of the head. In another type called *ardhavabhedaka*, pain appears in half of the head. At times headache starts in the morning and goes on increasing as the sun goes up in the sky till mid-day and then as sun comes down the pain also slows down. This type of headache is known as *suryavarta.* An acute type of headache which is very difficult for treatment is known as *anantavata.* In this type, the pain starts from the back of the head and migrates to the frontal as well as temporal regions. This is associated with redness and swelling in this region and is known as *shankhaka.*

Treatment : Different types of treatment are to be adopted for different types of headache. A medicine which is commonly used in all types of headache is *Anu taila.* This is a medicated oil prepared by boiling different medicinal plants in gingelly oil. About 20 drops of this medicated oil are to be dropped into each nostril and deeply inhaled. It is not poisonous. Therefore, while inhaling, if a portion of this oil goes to the stomach through the throat, it is not harmful. Deep inhalation of this oil may cause little irritation of the mucous membrane of the nose and this may result in sneezing. Even water may come out of the nose in large quantities. This oil, if properly inhaled, removes the blockage of the path from the sinuses to the nasal cavity. Removal of this blockage immediately relieves heaviness and mental strain. This oil also produces a soothing effect on the nerves. Normally this inhalation should be done only once. But if the headache is a chronic one or the patient is having acute attack of headache then this can be repeated, two to three times a day.

In *shlaishmika* type of headache *Lakshmi vilasa rasa* is very useful. This is available in the form of tablets of 0.25 gm. each. Two tablets of this should be taken three times a day mixed with honey. In *vatika* type of headache, *godanti bhasma* and *Shringa bhasma* are very useful. *Godanti* is calcium sulphate, and it is prepared in the form of a powder by a special pharmaceutical process. *Shringa* is the horn of deer. This is burnt into ashes by a special pharmaceutical process. These two powders are to be mixed in a dose of 0.25 gm. each, and taken mixed with honey three times daily.

In *paittika* type of headache, *Suvarna sutashekhara* is the medicine of choice. Among other components it contains gold in the form of a *bhasma*. It should be given in the dose of one tablet two times daily, on an empty stomach mixed with half teaspoon of cream and half teaspoon of sugar. If there is any difficulty in getting cream, then this medicine can be taken each time with a cup of milk mixed with sugar. The patient should be given a mild laxative periodically to keep him free from constipation.

Diet : Milk, sweet food and ghee are useful in this condition. Rice and soup prepared by boiling *kulattha* is also useful. Intake of hot milk especially that of the cow is considered to be exceedingly useful. The patient should avoid as far as possible fried things and spiced food articles.

Other regimens : The patient should avoid exposure to excessive heat, excessive cold or rain. He should not inhibit natural urges. If the headache is of *shlaishmika* type, the patient is well advised to keep short hair and avoid washing the head with cold water, as far as possible. Since mental strain and stress are important contributing factors for headache, the patient should be kept free from emotional factors like anxiety, anger and worry. He should not keep himself awake at night. Sleep during the day time is harmful.

MIGRAINE

This is a type of headache which is characterised by recurring paroxysmal attacks. It occurs in bouts. Often the patient gets pain only in one side of the head. Between the attacks, the patient feels perfectly well and leads a normal life.

In Ayurveda, this condition is known as *anantavarta*. There is another similar condition which is known as *suryavarta*. In this latter condition, the headache increases as the sun moves up in the sky, and the patient feels normal as the sun goes down.

Excessive worry and anxiety is considered to be the primary cause of this type of headache. Exposing the head to the heat of the sun or the cold wind or snow for a long time is one of the precipitating factors. Many patients suffering from migraine also suffer from sinusitis.

At times the headache become so intense that the patient gets vomiting. During the period between two attacks, the patient, no doubt, feels normal; but a trace of heaviness of head and congestion in the nose remains.

Treatment : If the patient is having nauseating sensation, it will be better to allow the patient to vomit out. Often indigestion precipitates the attacks of this disease. Vomiting relieves indigestion and thus, the patient is relieved of his headache. Even if there is no nausea, the patient should be made to drink 5-6 tumblerfuls of water and vomit it out. In a tumbler of water about half a teaspoon of salt should be added. It works better if lukewarm water is used for this purpose. After drinking water as much as possible, the throat of the patient should be tingled with the help of his own finger to induce vomiting and relieve the patient of his headache.

Such patients are usually constipated. They should be given *triphala* powder, one teaspoonful at bedtime with a cup of hot milk regularly.

A medicine which is very effective in this type of headache is *Anu taila*. This is medicated oil prepared by boiling 26 medicinal plants in gingelly oil and goat's milk. About 10 to 20 drops of this medicated oil is to be dropped into each nostril and deeply inhaled. It has no poisonous effect. Deep inhalation of the nose and cause sneezing. This oil, if properly inhaled, removes the blockage of the passage of the sinuses to the nose. The patient feels light in is head and the heaviness as well as mental strain is relieved. He gets good sleep and the nerves in the nasal passage are soothed. This inhalation therapy should be used 2-3 times a day. When the attack of the migraine is acute, use of this inhalation therapy gives instant relief to the patient.

Another medicated oil commonly used for treatment of migraine is known as *Shadbindu taila*. The dose of this oil is 6 drops only, and it is to be used as described before. This is prepared in mustard oil which is a little irritant to the mucous membrane of the nose, but it gives instant relief.

Suvarna sutashekhara is the drug of choice for the treatment of this condition. It contains mercury, gold, copper, sulphur and borax in *bhasma* form. Some poisonous drugs namely *vatsanabha* and *dhatura* are also used in this drug. But they are processed before they are added to the medicine and this processing makes them free from any adverse affect on the body. Ten more medicinal plants or drugs of animal origin are added to it and triturated with the juice of *bhringaraja*. This is given to the patient on empty stomach in a dose of 125 mg. twice daily with milk. It works both as a preventive, as well as curative for this condition. *Godanti bhasma,* which is very cheap. is also used for the treatment of this condition. This is given to the patient in a dose of one gm. three times a day, mixed with honey.

Diet : Fried things and spicy food articles are harmful to the patient. Curd and other sour things are also to be avoided. Cow's milk and cow's ghee are very useful for the patient suffering from migraine.

Other regimens : The patient should take care to keep himself free from indigestion, constipation, mental worries and anxieties and he should not expose himself to excessive heat, excessive cold and rain. He should go to bed early and avoid spending sleepless nights.

CHAPTER 16

AYURVEDIC MEDICINES FOR FAMILY PLANNING

IN ANCIENT India, large population was not a socio-economic problem. A couple without progeny was looked down with contempt, and it is common knowledge that earlier people scorned sterility. But more children were never considered an unmixed blessing. An incantation in the *Rigveda* had advanced the view: "A man with many children succumbs to miseries." This is perhaps the oldest statement with suggestion against a large family. To have one enlightened son is better than hundreds of illiterates. Like the solitary moon, the former strives and removes darkness which is not possible by hundred of stars. It is with this in view, Lopamudra wanted to have only one virtuous son in preference to hundreds of undesirable ones.

In ancient classics on religion, medicine and sexology, much emphasis was laid upon the preservation of *shukra* or seminal fluid. Semen, when preserved in the body through the process of *brahmacharya* (celibacy) promotes strength, complexion, longevity and the power of resistance to disease and decay. Except for the sole purpose of procreation, sexual union was proscribed. Sexual act is a part of *dharma* or religious duty which is to be performed following the prescribed procedure.

For those who are unable to adopt these religious prescriptions and prohibitions, several natural including mechanical devices are described in Ayurvedic works and works on sexology.

Some (non-poisonous) local and oral contraceptives described in these books are elaborated below :

(a) In *Yogaratnakara* and *Brihad-yoga-tarangini*, the woman is asked to get her genital tract fumigated with the smoke of margosa wood by burning it. This is to be done after the stoppage of her menstrual flow. This is prescribed to prevent conception. In *Tantrasara sangraha,* this reference occurs in a slightly different way. The fumigation is suggested to be done during the period or *ritu,* the menstrual period or the period of fertilisation.

A very common technique which is even now practiced in certain parts of the globe for contraception is also described in *Yogaratnakara, Brihad-yoga-tarangini* and *Brihannighantu ratnakara*. A piece of rock salt smeared with sesame oil should be kept in the vaginal tract of the female before coitus to prevent conception. In *Brihad-yoga-tarangini,* there is another reference in this connection. After coitus, a tampon consisting of rock salt and oil should be inserted into the vaginal tract which will work as a contraceptive. *Rasa-ratna-samuchchaya* has elucidated the mechanism of action of rock-salt in preventing conception. According to it, the *shukra* or sperm gets dissolved or broken into pieces by coming into contact with rock-salt smeared with oil. This will not stop menstruation but will only prevent conception, even during the time of fertility. By implication, this local contraceptive does not in any way affect the ovulation process of the woman but incapacitates sperm which otherwise would have got united with the ovum to cause pregnancy. According to *Haramekhala,* a piece of rock-salt smeared with oil and kept at the mouth of the uterus, *garbhashaya vadana,* i.e., cervix helps in preventing conception.

A paste prepared with the seeds of *palasha* (*Butea monosperma*), honey and ghee be kept inside the vagina in sufficient quantity. This is described in *Brihad-yoga-tarangini* to prevent conception. Another reading of the concerned verse is available in *Bharata-bhaishajya-ratnakara,* according to which a very fine paste is required to be made probably with a view to prevent any irritation in the female genital tract. According to *Haramekhala,* this medicine is to be applied in the vagina during the time of fertilisation. According to the commentators on *Haramekhala,* this medicine should be applied during the entire period of fertilisation and not only once with a view to prevent conception.

(b) *Oral Contraceptives for Males* : In ancient classics on sexology and medicine, oral drugs for producing sterility in males are also mentioned. One such reference is in *Ratirahasya*, according to which, if an individual takes the powder of *haridra* or *rajani* (*Curcuma longa*) impregnated with goat's urine, he becomes sterile. This recipe is said to produce its effect instantaneously even on young people. In *Rasa-prakasha-sudhakara*, one complete chapter, is devoted to the description of various formulae for *bijabandha* (prevention of the ejaculation of semen) during coitus.

(c) *Oral Contraceptives for Females*; The following formulae are described to produce sterility in females :

(i) *Old Sugar-Candy* : In *Tantra-sara-sangruha*, old sugar-candy with milk is described to be used orally to prevent conception. In *Bhavaprakasha*, *Balatanta*, *Kuchimaratantra*, *Yogaratnakara* and *Brihannighantu ratnakara*, old sugar-candy is suggested to be taken. In *Anangaranga* and *Panchasayaka*, details of this type of recipe are given.

In *Balatantra*, there is yet another reference to sugar-candy being taken with rice-wash in the form of a linctus to produce sterility in the woman without affecting her sexual passion. This is a popularly used recipe in the villages.

(ii) *Root of chitraka*: In *Kuchimaratantra* and *Anangaranga*, root of *chitraka* (*Plumbago zeylanica*) is described to be boiled with rice-wash, and after filteration, the decoction is to be taken consecutively for three days after the stoppage of the menstrual flow. This is stated to make the woman barren. In *Panchasayaka*, this decoction is said to make the woman barren forever.

(iii) *Fruit of kadamba*: The fruit of *kadamba* (*Anthocephalus indicus*) added with honey, one fourth in quantity, if taken for three days along with hot water, produces sterility in the woman. This is described in *Anangaranga.* According to *Panchasayaka*, however, the fruit of *kadamba* is to be taken with honey and rice-wash for three days after the stoppage of the menstrual flow.

(iv) *Seed of Sarshapa*: In *Anangaranga, sarshapa (Brassica compestris)* when taken for seven days during the period of fertilisation along with rice-wash as vehicle, causes sterility in the woman. In *Panchasayaka*, a very small quantity of *sarshapa* is stated to be taken and the rice-wash is stated to be prepared of white variety of rice only.

In *Kuchimaratantra,* rice grains and sugar are mentioned to be added to *sarshapa.* All these three in equal quantities should be mixed with rice-wash and taken by the woman to stop menstruation.

In *Brihad-yoga-tarangini, sarshapa* is mentioned to be taken after triturating with gingelly oil for three days during menstrual period. This will prevent conception.

(v) *Seeds of palasha*: In *Yogachintamani,* a recipe for producing sterility is given. Seeds of *palasha* (*Butea monosperma*) are to be powdered and taken with water for three days during the time of fertilisation.

In *Panchasayaka,* fruit of *kshirivriksha* (*Mimusops hexandra*) and the flower of *shalmali* (*Salmalia malbarica*) are described to be added to seeds of *palasha* and then taken with alcohol for 15 days for producing sterility in the woman. Another version of this verse is also available, according to which ghee is to be used in the place of alcohol and there is no mention of time-limit for the intake of this recipe.

In *Garudapurana*, seed of this tree is stated to be made into a paste by adding honey and then taken by the woman during her menstrual period. This will prevent both menstruation and conception in future. In *Yogaratna-samuchchaya*, there is no mention of the prevention of conception by the intake of this recipe. Only the stoppage of menstruation is described there as its effect.

(vi) *Flower of Japa*: Flower of *japa* (*Hibiscus rosa-sinensis*) is described in *Bhavaprakasha, Brihannighanta ratnakara, Balatantra* and *Yogaratnakara* to produce sterility in the woman.

In *Brihad-yoga-tarangini*, there is an interesting observation in this connection. The recipe, if taken during the time of delivery of a child is stated to prevent future conception and, if at all there is conception, the foetus will not grow; by implication, there will be an abortion.

(vii) *Root of Tanduliyaka* : Administration of the root of *tanduliyaka* (*Amaranthus spinosus*), made into a paste by adding rice-wash, to a woman after her menstruation for three days will make her sterile. This is described in *Yogaratnakara, Brihad-yogatarangini* and *Brihannighanta ratnakara*.

(viii) *Haridra*: One piece of the rhizome of haridra (*Curcuma longa*) should be taken every day, for six days (three days during menses and three days thereafter). This is described in *Kuchimaratantra* to produce sterility in the woman but she will continue to have menses.

(ix) *Trapusa* (*Cucumis sativus*) Intake of the paste prepared of the leaves of *shelu* (*Cordia dichotoma*) is described in *Bhaishajya ratnavali* to stop menstruation.

(x) *Leaves of Patha* : After taking the purificatory bath after menstruation, if the woman takes the leaves of patha (*Cissampelos pareira*) she will not conceive.

(xi) *Flower of shalmali*: In *Tantra sara sangraha*, intake of the flower of *shalmali* (*Salmalia malabarica*) is stated to cause sterility.

(xii) *Fruit of Bakula* : Fruit of *bakula* (*Mimusops elengi*) made into a paste by grinding with alcohol, if taken during the period of menstruation, will stop menstruation in future.

(xiii) *Maricha* (*Piper nigrum*) : In *Yoga-ratna-samuchchaya*, the paste of white variety of *maricha* (*Piper nigrum*) made with sugar water, if taken for three days during menstruation, is described to stop future menstruation.

(xiv) *Leaves of Champaka* : Leaves of *Champaka* (*Michelia champaca*) are to be soaked in water overnight and made to a paste. If administered to the lady during the period of her menstruation, this will prevent conception. The period in years for which this contraceptive remains effective coincides with the number of leaves taken as per the method described above.

(xv) *Leaf of Tala* : Powder of tala (*Borassus flaberllifer*) leaf mixed with red ochre, if taken with cold water on the fourth day of menstrual period, is described to cause sterility.

(xvi) *Gunja* (*Abrus precatorius*) : A very common and popularly used recipe for contraception is the white variety of *gunja* (*Abrus precatorius*). Different methods of administration of this drug are prevalent in different parts of the country. Some people use the entire seed and some others use only the cotyledons removing the epicarp after soaking it in water for one night. Administration of one *gunja* (white variety) on the fourth fay of menstruation, two on the fifth day and three on the sixth day is stated to prevent conception for three years.

(xvii) *Castor seeds* (*Ricinus communis*) : Administration of the pulp of one or two castor seeds during the menstrual period is stated to prevent fertilisation for one and two years respectively.

(xviii) *Agnimantha*: Administration of a decoction prepared with the root-bark of *agnimantha* (*Clerodendrum phlomidis*) together with rice-wash is mentioned to cause sterility.

(xix) *Flowers of jambu*: Flowers of *jambu* (*Syzygium cumini*) triturated with the urine of the cow are stated to cause sterility in the woman when taken during the time of menstruation.

(xx) *Old ghee* : Intake of three-year-old ghee for 15 days makes the woman sterile. Cow's ghee is commonly used for this purpose.

(xxi) *Talisha* : Leaf of *talisha* (*Abies webbiana*) mixed with equal quantity of *gairika* (ochre) is described in *Yogaratnakara* and *Brihad-yoga-tarangini* to produce sterility in the woman.

(xxii) *Badari* (*Zizyphus jujuba*) : After menses, if a woman takes *badari* (*Zizyphus jujuba*) and lac boiled in gingelly oil, she would not conceive.

(xxiii) *Pippalyadi churna* : *Pippali* (*Piper longum*), *vidanga* (*Embelia ribes*) and *tankana* (borax), made to a powder in equal quantities and if taken with milk during the period of fertilisation, there will be no conception. This recipe is described in *Bhavaprakasha*, *Yogaratnakara* and *Brihannighantu ratnakara*.

(xxiv) *Dhatryadi churna* : In *Bhaishajya-ratnavali*, the powder of *dhatri* (*Emblica officinalis*), *arjuna* (*Terminalia arjuna*) and *abhaya* (*Terminalia chebula*) is described to stop menstruation if taken with water.

(xxv) *Rasanjanadi Churna* : A powder prepared of *rasanjana* (aqueous extract of *Berberis aristata*), *haimavati* (*Acorus calamus*) and *haritaki* (*Terminalia chebula*), if taken with cold water, is described to stop menstruation. Obviously there will be no conception.

(xxvi) *Krishnajitakadi vati* : In *Kuchimaratantra*, a recipe is mentioned to produce sterility and stop menstruation in the woman. This is made of *kala jira* (*Carum carvi*), *kachura* (*Curucuma zedoaria*), *nagakeshara* (*Mesua ferrea*), *kalaunji* (*Nigella sativa*) and *katphala* (*Myrica nagi*), taken in equal quantities. Powders of these ingredients are triturated by adding water, and then made into pills.

(xxvii) *Chandanadi churna* : Powders of sandalwood, mustard and sugar are to be taken in equal quantities. It should be mixed with rice-wash and administered to make the woman sterile.

(xxviii) *Kutajadi churna* : The woman who drinks in wine, the fruits of *kutaja* (*Holarrhena antidysenterica*), *kadamba* (*Anthocephalus indicus*), *balaka* (*Valeriana wallichii*) and *chandana* (*Santalum album*) becomes sterile.

Some of the above mentioned recipes are single drugs and some are compound preparations. Most of these preparations are of vegetable origin. In some compound preparations, minerals are also added. Some of these recipes are mentioned in the classics on medicines and sexology and some others do not find a mention therein but are extensively used by people out of experience accumulated since centuries. The choice of recipes for different types of individuals depends upon their age and physical constitution.

APPENDICES

APPENDIX 1

(Medicinal Plants, etc., described in the text)

APPENDIX II
(Recipes described in the text)

APPENDIX III
(Index of Technical Terms)

Notes

Notes

Notes